A Little Book of
Latin Love Poetry

A Little Book of Latin Love Poetry

A Transitional Reader for Catullus, Horace, and Ovid

by

JOHN BREUKER and MARDAH B. C. WEINFIELD

Bolchazy-Carducci Publishers, Inc.
Wauconda, Illinois USA

General Editors:
Marie Carducci Bolchazy
Laurie Haight Keenan

Cover Design & Typography:
Adam Phillip Velez

Cartography:
The Ohio University Cartographic Center

A Little Book of Latin Love Poetry
A Transitional Reader for Catullus, Horace, and Ovid

John Breuker & Mardah B. C. Weinfield

Latin Texts:
CATULLUS: *Catullus, Tibullus and Pervigilium Veneris.* Edited and translated by F. W. Cornish, J. B. Postgate, and J. W. Mackail. The Loeb Classical Library. Cambridge, Mass.: Harvard University Press, 1962. HORACE: *Horace. Odes and Epodes.* Edited and translated by C. E. Bennett. The Loeb Classical Library. Cambridge, Mass.: 1968. OVID: *Ovid. Heroides and Amores.* Edited and translated by G. Showerman. The Loeb Classical Library. Cambridge, Mass.: 1958. The Loeb Classical Library ® is a registered trademark of the President and Fellows of Harvard College.

Bolchazy-Carducci Publishers, Inc.
1000 Brown Street, Unit 101
Wauconda, Illinois 60084
www.bolchazy.com

Printed in the United States of America
2006
by United Graphics

ISBN-13: 978-0-86516-601-1
ISBN-10: 0-86516-601-3

Library of Congress Cataloging-in-Publication Data

A little book of Latin love poetry : a transitional reader for Catullus,
    Horace, and Ovid / by John Breuker and Mardah B. C. Weinfield.
        p. cm.
    Includes bibliographical references.
    ISBN-13: 978-0-86516-601-1 (pbk. : alk. paper)
    ISBN-10: 0-86516-601-3 (pbk. : alk. paper)
    1. Love poetry, Latin. 2. Latin language--Readers--Poetry.
I. Catullus, Gaius Valerius. II. Horace. III. Ovid, 43 B.C.-17 or 18
A.D. IV. Breuker, John. V. Weinfield, Mardah B. C.
PA6135.L68L58 2006
871'.01083543--dc22
                                                2006017353

CONTENTS

PREFACE

Our goal in writing *A Little Book of Latin Love Poetry* (hereafter *Libellus*) is to introduce students, generally at the third/fourth semester high school level or the late second/early third semester college level, to mainstream Latin poets and to ease their transition to reading these authors. To this end, our reader contains passages of both modified and authentic Latin verse. We have modified carefully selected Latin passages in order to make them more accessible to beginning readers (see paragraph 4). When combined with the extensive vocabulary and reading support provided, the modified passages provide a bridge from syntax, grammar, vocabulary and individual sentences (the elements of reading) to the coherent whole of connected authentic Latin literature (the actuality of reading). The unmodified passages, used as review, contain further annotation and provide familiarity with authentic Latin texts and meters. These unmodified passages enable the teacher and student to address literary, metrical, humanistic, philological and comprehension concerns beyond those already introduced in connection with the modified texts. As much as possible, we have attempted to align the content and presentation of material with the Standards for Classical Language Learning.

The *Libellus* addresses in a very direct manner Goals 1, 3 and 5 in their entirety. If one considers a poem a "product" of the Romans, then Goal 2.2 is also addressed directly. Goals 2.1 and 4.2 are approached indirectly in the Introductions to the authors and lend themselves to projects outside of class at the discretion and wish of the teacher. Goal 4.1 in also approached indirectly throughout the *Libellus*, and directly in several Rapid Reviews, some FYIs (e.g. p. 77), and in the Major Reviews.

The Latin passages focus on a theme prevalent in the Roman world and our own: Love. We chose this theme to capture the interest of students and because it resonates throughout the works of Rome's major authors. The authors included—Catullus, Horace and Ovid—were selected because in most curricula they are among the first to be read following the acquisition of fundamental vocabulary and the syntactical/grammatical bases essential to reading.

We have chosen to modify the Latin Passages because, in our experience, students new to reading authentic Latin literature are often overwhelmed by the multiple tasks they must perform simultaneously. When reading, students must deal with issues of vocabulary, syntax/grammar, unfamiliar forms, word order, and—in poetry—meter and figures of speech. This *Libellus* addresses these issues in the following ways:

1) Extensive reading vocabulary accompanies each passage, together with a full glossary in the back of the book. A few unusual words have been replaced with more common ones.

2) Reading Helps address issues of syntax/grammar and form. Rapid Reviews address syntax/grammar which many students find problematical.

3) Modified Latin delays issues of poetic word order and metrical considerations until the unit review.

4) Poetic devices are included and defined, where appropriate, <u>throughout</u> the *Libellus*.

It is our intent that this transitional reader will fuse components of both the inductive and deductive methodologies that permeate the classrooms of the twenty-first century, and that it will be of particular use in standards-based learning and assessment. We also believe that this volume will make starting to read Latin literature more pleasurable and less onerous for students, thus increasing their appreciation of Rome's contributions to our literary and humanistic heritage.

We gratefully acknowledge significant encouragement received during this endeavor. Lou and Marie Bolchazy from Bolchazy-Carducci Publishers initiated the project and shepherded it at each stage to its conclusion. Our editor, Laurie Haight Keenan, provided countless incisive suggestions and an eagle eye for detail. The Trustees of Western Reserve Academy and its Headmaster, Dr. Henry E. Flanagan, awarded a sabbatical leave and generously provided an additional academic year released from classroom obligations to enable continued writing. Congenial colleagues around the country cooperated in field-testing preliminary drafts; without their generous spirit and suggestions for improvement a far less effective version would have resulted. Any remaining infelicities or errors are our responsibility. Finally, and most of all, our spouses have been understanding, supportive and patient to a degree far beyond the norm. To one and all we address the words of appreciation spoken by Trojan Aeneas to Queen Dido for the Carthaginians' warm welcome to his storm-tossed voyagers:

> *grātēs persolvere dignās/nōn opis est nostrae.*
> To offer deserved thanks is not within our power.
>   Vergil, *Aeneid* I.600–601

JOHN BREUKER, JR.
MARDAH B. C. WEINFIELD

NOTES TO STUDENTS

We have organized this *Libellus* to provide students with maximum support as they begin the process of reading and interpreting authentic Latin texts. For unmodified Latin text, we have selected the Loeb versions, and it is from these that we then created the modified Latin versions.

We have altered the authentic text in four ways. First, we have rearranged the word order into more easily recognized thought units ("chunks"). Second, we have simplified some vocabulary, grammatical forms and constructions, as needed. Third, we have sometimes omitted one or more lines of difficult authentic text. Finally, we have at times changed punctuation or spelling. Because of these changes, the modified versions lose some of their metrical quality (i.e. they do not completely scan). The unmodified text for each selection appears in the Unit Review, where a Textual Matters section highlights significant differences between the modified and unmodified texts. This is an appropriate time to consider meter and scansion. A brief discussion of metrics is found in **Appendix C**.

We introduce each author with a concise biography and, in addition, we briefly summarize and describe in context each Latin selection. Regarding the authors, we recognize that each writer may be understood in two ways—as he really was and as his literary *persōna* (his mask) indicates. We devote a section of each biography to a description of that author's *persōna*, but for the sake of clarity we have chosen to minimize our presentation of this topic in the selection summaries.

To aid in the reading of each Latin selection, students will find extensive Vocabulary and Reading Helps on each left-hand page, designed to address issues associated with the Latin text which stands opposite on the right-hand page. In the Reading Helps, we have at times deliberately posed questions. We did so for two reasons: 1) to help the students decipher important clues for understanding the text, and 2) to show the students the kind of mental questions they should be asking themselves as they read a Latin passage. With each question, we try to make its answer apparent. For any vocabulary words not listed opposite the Latin text, a full glossary/dictionary is located at the back of the volume.

Under each modified selection is a list of questions, which we have created to aid in the understanding and interpretation of the selection's text. We have included questions of two types: 1) Analysis and Comprehension of the Latin Text, and 2) Literary Analysis and Discussion.

1. Questions analyzing the Latin text are those which ask about matters of vocabulary and/or syntax so that the student will be able to read/translate the Latin text accurately: Is the *ut* clause indicating purpose or result? Does the *cum* indicate manner or accompaniment? How can one decide if *vēnī* is a singular, present imperative form of *veniō* or a 1st person, singular, perfect, active, indicative form of the verb? Comprehension questions are those which, based upon accurate textual analysis, check on the reader's understanding of a passage's meaning/content: What is the antecedent of this pronoun? How many characters appear in this poem? What four physical characteristics does the passage give for character A?

2. Literary Analysis and Discussion: questions, based upon accurate analysis and comprehension of the Latin text, which deal with the passage as literature to be interpreted, suggest topics for discussion in the classroom or for interpretation in a short essay, or ask the student's opinion based upon his/her understanding of the passage: What impact does the sight of A have upon B? What is ambiguous about the poet's word choice of _____? How does the poet's use of a poetic figure (e.g. onomatopoeia) enhance the passage's literary quality? Why, based upon your reading of the passage, do you think the poet does this, but not that?

There are also questions in the Unit Review, where the student will find Points to Ponder for each unmodified selection. These questions generally are more open-ended and broader in nature, designed to help the student draw connections among the various selections, and among the authors as well.

Following each modified selection is a Rapid Review of a particular grammatical or syntactical topic associated with that selection. The information contained in the Rapid Reviews is based upon the grammars of Gildersleeve and Bennett, and the dictionary of Traupman, all of which are available in paperbook editions from Bolchazy-Carducci Publishers. Our expectation is that a teacher choosing to use this book will have these references available for students' use. This *Libellus*, however, does contain an Appendix (**Appendix D**) of essential forms, syntax and grammar.

We recognize that not *all* the review material will necessarily have been studied by *all* students, but the reviews *have* been designed to include material covered by *most* high school students at the end of the third semester, and by *most* college students at the end of the second semester. Since our book strives to ease the transition from a basic textbook to reading authentic authors for students from a wide background of methodologies, we wish to emphasize that we expect the students using our books to have a comfortable grasp of the topics of grammar, morphology and syntax recommended to be covered by these semester/year benchmarks in the latest professional discussions of standards. (Chapter 11 in S. Davis, *Latin in American Schools. Teaching the Ancient World.* Atlanta, 1991, especially pp. 54–58, and Chapter 5: "National Standards and Curriculum Guidelines" by M. G. Abbott, S. Davis and R. C. Gascoyne in R. A. LaFleur (ed), *Latin for the 21st Century. From Concept to Classroom.* Glenville, IL, 1998, especially pp. 52–56. See the Addendum on the following page for a sample listing of the syntax topics.)

We also recognize that many of the topics which these lists specify are so thoroughly familiar to almost all students as to need no review. We have chosen as Rapid Review (RR) topics, therefore, those which our own teaching experiences have shown to be problematic for many students. Generally speaking, these topics are covered in the second high school year or second college semester. The following topics are reviewed in this *Libellus*, as they are met in the context of a selected passage:

RR 1: temporal clauses
RR 2: vocatives and imperatives
RR 3: correlative pairings
RR 4: formation of the present tense of the subjunctive mood
RR 5: five uses of the tricky word *quam*
RR 6: interrogative pronouns and adjectives
RR 7: enclitics
RR 8: comparison of adjectives
RR 9: conditional sentences
RR 10: deponent verbs
RR 11: irregular verbs
RR 12: the formation and comparison of adverbs
RR 13: demonstrative adjectives/pronouns

Each Rapid Review includes practice exercises on its topic and, in addition, the *Libellus* contains two Major Reviews, one of infinitive forms and usages, and one of participle forms and usages. Each Major Review includes multiple exercises for practice with each substantive section of the review. We have chosen not to emphasize a review of subjunctive forms and usages because there are relatively few to be found in the passages which appear in this volume.

ADDENDUM |||||||||||||||||||||||||||||||||||||||||||||||||||||||||||||||||||||||||||||||||||||||||||||||||||||||||||||||||||||||||||||||||||||||||||||||

Though the pages cited on the previous page in the works of Davis and LaFleur discuss, *inter alia*, topics of grammar, morphology and syntax, only items of syntax are listed here as examples.

Depending on the texts used and pace of the program, items marked with an asterisk (*) are sometimes taught later than here indicated.

Level 1 First Year (Schools), First Semester (Colleges/Universities)

Syntax

Nominative case: subject, predicate noun/nominative and adjective (with linking verbs)

Genitive case: possession

Dative case: indirect object, *with special adjectives

Accusative case: direct object, object of preposition, place to which

Ablative case: object of preposition, accompaniment, means, manner, time when, *agent, *absolute

Vocative case: direct address

Level 2 Second Year (Schools), Second Semester (Colleges/Universities)

Syntax

Genitive case: whole/partitive

Dative case: *agent, purpose, possession, compound verbs

Accusative case: subject of infinitive, extent (of space), duration (of time)

Ablative case: separation, comparison, special verbs, respect/specification, cause, degree of difference

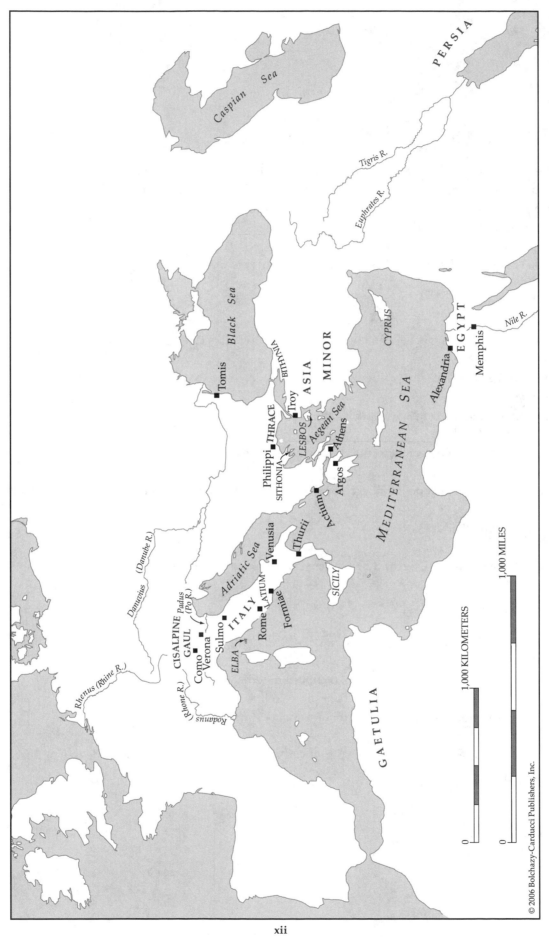

Places Mentioned in *A Little Book of Latin Love Poetry*

© 2006 Bolchazy-Carducci Publishers, Inc.

INTRODUCTION TO CATULLUS

The person who, according to established literary tradition, was known as Gaius Valerius Catullus was born about 85 BCE in Verona, an important town in Cisalpine Gaul. His family seems to have been quite prosperous and influential. They are reported to have hosted such important Roman guests as the provincial governor Metellus and an up-and-coming aristocrat named Gaius Julius Caesar. The century's early years were a tumultuous period of social upheaval, political turmoil and civil war in Rome. Catullus therefore would have lived during the power of military strongmen such as Sulla. The poet also would have known of the lawlessness associated with published proscription lists; he would have heard of the bitter political enmity between Rome's *populārēs* and its *optimātēs*; and he would have observed the decline of traditional values in the family, the community and religion.

J. Caesar

The youthful Catullus went to Rome to further his educational and career opportunities, and soon became part of a set of young social and artistic sophisticates. The youthful poets were rather disparagingly referred to as the *poētae novī* and the *neoteroi* by Cicero and others of the "establishment." The writers included Catullus, Caecilius, Calvus, Cinna, and Gallus, among others, all gathered around an influential *grammaticus* named Valerius Cato.

These budding artists appreciated the early (seventh-century BCE) Greek lyric poets Alcaeus and Sappho for their highly personalized poetry. The young men wrote about such topics such as their passionate desire, their love of political freedom, their personal lives, the pain of death and their grief over it. But the *poētae novī* also were attracted to the artistic ideals of the third-century Hellenistic Greek poets from Alexandria, Egypt. At the famous Library located there, talented poets like Callimachus and Theocritus stressed brevity, learnedness, polish and wit as key features of good poetry.

Sappho & Alcaeus

Catullus and his friends apparently valued features and topics similar to those valued in this Greek poetry. Admirable **poetry** was to be crisp, even racy, filled with everyday, colloquial words used in fresh new ways. The goal was a *carmen* (poem) that was *novum* (new), *doctum* (learned), *expolītum* (polished), *labōriōsum* (carefully reworked and revised), *breve* (short), *lepidum* (smoothly wrought and seamlessly organized) and *venustum* (charming). Admirable **people** likewise were to be urbane, polite, sophisticated, witty and learned. Consequently, his poems deal with people and their behavior. He writes about his friends, enemies, lovers and rivals. He comments upon what is acceptable, unacceptable, expected, deviant, provincial [or rustic], urbane, the comic and the tragic.

We have 113 of Catullus' poems. In them, the reader meets an author passionate about love, life and poetry. Catullus also presents the reader with several *persōnae* (masks): at times he writes with racy vulgarity, then refined charm, soon a bold obscenity, next sophisticated wit, all an intriguing blend of subjective engagement with ironic detachment. In twenty-five poems he chronicles the agony and ecstasy of his torrid love affair with a more experienced married woman whom he chooses to call Lesbia. The second-century CE writer Apuleius identifies her as Clodia, the notorious widow of the consular Metellus mentioned in the opening paragraph. She was a sister (and alleged incestuous partner) of the political strong man P. Clodius Pulcher. SELECTIONS I–VI are from these amatory poems.

When he was in his late twenties, Catullus apparently served for a year on the governor's staff in Bithynia, a part of Asia Minor on the southern coast of the Black Sea. He died a few years after his return to Italy; St. Jerome reports that his death occurred in 54 BCE.

TIMELINE FOR CATULLUS

? 85/84 BCE ?	C.'s birth in Verona
? 62 BCE ?	C. in Rome
? 61 BCE ?	C. meets Clodia
? 58 BCE ?	C. in Bithynia
? 54 BCE ?	C. dies

Catullus (?) reciting poetry

CATULLUS SELECTIONS

Catullus (?) recites to a rapt audience

Catullus 51.1–12 Modified

READING VOCABULARY

Line 1 **pār – pār, (pāris)** (+ dative): equal, like

2 **fās est** – "it is (divinely) allowed (lawful, right)"

superāre – superō, superāre, superāvī, superātum: be above, surpass

3 **adversus – adversus, -a, -um:** turned toward, facing, opposite

identidem – *adv.*: repeatedly, again and again

4 **dulce – dulcis, -e:** sweet, pleasant

rīdentem – rīdeō, rīdēre, rīsī, rīsum: laugh, smile

6 **nam** – *conj.*: for

aspexī – aspiciō, aspicere, aspexī, aspectum: look at, behold, lay eyes on

7 **ōre – ōs, ōris,** *n.*: mouth; pl. face, countenance

superest – supersum, superesse, superfuī, superfutūrus: be left over, to survive

8 **torpet – torpeō, torpēre, torpuī, _____:** be paralyzed or numb

9 **tenuis – tenuis, -e:** thin, slender

artus – artus, -ūs, *m.*: joint, limb

dēmānat – dēmānō, dēmānāre, dēmānāvī, _____: run/drip down, trickle, flow, spread

10 **tintinnant – tintinnō, tintinnāre, _____, _____:** make a ringing sound, to ring

11 **teguntur – tegō, tegere, texī, tectum:** cover

READING HELPS

Latin, like other languages, has many contractions, synonyms, and idiomatic, poetic or colloquial expressions. Several of these are found in this opening selection.

Line 1 *Ille* is a demonstrative adjective used substantively as the subject of *vidētur*.

mī (cf. lines 2 and 7) is a common contraction of *mihi*.

vidētur: The passive voice of *videō* often has the meaning of "seem" and patterns with a predicate noun/adjective or, as here, a complementary infinitive (*esse* and *superāre*).

2 *dīvōs* is a synonym for the more common noun *deōs*.

3 *sedēns*, modifying *quī*, and *ridentem* (in line 4), modifying *tē*, are present active participles. See Major Review #2 if the topic of participles is unfamiliar.

4 *dulce* is an "adverbial accusative," an accusative form used as a positive degree adverb: "sweetly."

5 The relative pronoun *quod* has an "understood" antecedent, and consequently means "a thing which . . ."

The phrase *mihi miserō* is a clear example of the poetic "dative of separation" replacing the more common "ablative of separation."

6 *simul atque*, introducing a temporal clause here, means "as soon as."

7 The phrase *nihil vōcis* illustrates the colloquial "genitive of the whole/partitive genitive" construction. "Nothing of a voice" really means "no voice."

11 The final line is a vivid reminder that this is modified poetry, for the poet employs METONYMY twice in this line. METONYMY is the poetic device by which a poet uses one word for another it suggests. Here, the *lūmina*, "lights" of the body, suggest the eyes. What then does *geminā nocte*, "twin (or two-fold) night," suggest?

FOR YOUR INFORMATION (hereafter merely FYI)

Line 2 The indeclinable noun *fās* conveys a very different idea from *lex* or *iūs*. The distinctions will become more clear if the differences among nefarious acts, illegal acts and unjust acts are considered.

Line 5 Poets sometimes use a "dative of agent" where prose writers use an "ablative of agent" too.

Line 6 When *atque* appears after *simul, aequē, īdem* or *pariter*, it means "as."

Line 7 Similar to the phrase *nihil vōcis*, consider the phrases *satis pecuniae, nimis stultitiae, multum aquae, parum frumentī* or *plūs virtūtis*.

Line 10 *Caveat lector!!!* ("Let the reader beware!!!") The declensional endings help distinguish *auris, -is*, f. ("ear") from *aura, -ae*, f. ("breeze") and *aurum, -ī*, n. ("gold").

Catullus 51.1–12 Modified

This poem follows the text of a Greek poem by Sappho, a poet in the seventh century BCE, who lived on the island of Lesbos off the coast of Asia Minor. Catullus pays tribute to Sappho by using "Lesbia" as a pseudonym for his own object of desire, believed by many scholars to be Clodia, a patrician woman with a notorious reputation (cf. **Introduction**). She has been variously associated with the corruption of young men (in particular M. Caelius Rufus), with religious impropriety, and with the exile of Cicero.

Sappho

Many readers consider this poem the first in Catullus' cycle of poems to Lesbia. In the text below, Catullus describes a man sitting opposite Lesbia, but focuses upon the poet's own physical reactions to her presence.

> Ille mī pār esse deō vidētur,
> ille, sī fās est, mī superāre dīvōs vidētur,
> quī sedēns adversus identidem tē spectat
> et tē dulce rīdentem audit,
> 5   quod omnēs sensūs mihi miserō ēripit:
>
> nam simul atque tē, Lesbia, aspexī,
> nihil vōcis mī in ōre superest
> sed lingua torpet,
> tenuis flamma sub artūs dēmānat,
> 10   aurēs sonitū suō tintinnant,
> et lūmina mea gemīnā nocte teguntur.

ANALYSIS AND COMPREHENSION OF THE LATIN TEXT

(See **Notes to Students** for information about the differences between the various types of questions)

1. To whom does the demonstrative adjective *ille* in lines 1–2 refer? the personal pronouns *mī/mihi* in lines 1, 2, 5 and 7? and *tē* in lines 3, 4, and 6?

2. Identify the antecedents of the relative pronouns *quī* in line 3 and *quod* in line 5.

LITERARY ANALYSIS AND DISCUSSION

1. What impact does the text suggest the sight of Lesbia has upon the poet? Is this description meant to be taken seriously, or is it an exaggeration? If it is the latter, the poet is employing HYPERBOLE to heighten or exaggerate the dramatic effect, another poetic technique (cf. METONYMY in the Reading Help for line 11).

RAPID REVIEW #1: TEMPORAL CLAUSES

See Bennett, 287–293 and/or Gildersleeve, 559–588 for a more detailed discussion of this topic.

As their name implies, temporal clauses add the adverbial idea of time to a sentence. The most common introductory conjunctions, all followed by a verb in the indicative mood, are:

postquam: after
ut, ubī, cum: when
simul atque (ac), cum prīmum: as soon as
antequam, priusquam: before
dum, dōnec, quoad: while, as long as

PRACTICE

Translate these contextual sentences. The first five are based on SELECTION I, the last five on SELECTIONs II–XI.

1. Postquam tē aspexī, nihil vōcis mī in ōre superfuit.
2. Ubi ille vir adversus te sēdit, omnēs sensūs mī miserō ēreptī sunt.
3. Simul atque tē, Lesbia, dulce ridentem audīvī, mea lingua torpuit.
4. Antequam lumina mea geminā nocte teguntur, tenuis flamma sub artūs meōs demānat.
5. Dum lingua mea torpet, aurēs sonitū suō tintinnant.
6. Cum nostra brevis lux occidit, nox perpetua ūna dormienda est.
7. Dōnec tibi grātus eram, beātior Persārum rēge fuī.
8. Sōl revenit ubī nox abiit.
9. Ut puella ante oculōs nostrōs stetit, nullam mendam in eius corpore vīdī.
10. Cum multa mīlia basiōrum fēcerimus, illa conturbābimus.

Catullus 43.1–4, 6–8 Modified

READING VOCABULARY

Line 1 **nāsō – nāsus, -ī,** *m.:* nose

2 **bellō – bellus, -a, -um:** pretty, charming, handsome

nigrīs – niger, -gra, -grum: dark, black

ocellīs – a diminuitive form of *oculīs,* **from oculus, -ī,** *m.:* little eye

3 **digitīs – digitus, -ī,** *m.:* finger

ōre – as in SELECTION I, line 7: os, ōris, *n.:* mouth

siccō – siccus -a, -um: dry, arid, parched

4 **sanē –** *adv.:* really, indeed, to be sure

nimis – *adv.:* too, excessively

7 **saeculum – saeculum, -ī,** *n.:* age, generation

insapiēns – insapiēns (insapientis): unwise, tasteless

infacētum – infacētus, -a, -um: dull, crude, lacking wit/humor; witless, clueless

READING HELPS

Line 1 Be sure to analyze the verb form *salvē.* Once that is done, the case of *puella* will be obvious.

1–4 Remember that the "genitive of quality/description" is generally used when one is mentioning non-physical characteristics (e.g. a person *of keen intellect*) while the "ablative of quality/description" is used with physical characteristics (e.g. a person *of great strength*). Does Catullus follow this general pattern here?

5 The "long" ē and the question mark clarify whether *tēne* is a form of the verb *teneō* or of the personal pronoun *tū,* with an interrogative enclitic (*-ne*) attached. cf. *Venīsne?* "Are you coming?"

6 Remember that the preposition *cum* ("with") is attached as an enclitic to the end of ablative case forms of personal pronouns. See Rapid Review #6, 3.

FYI

Line 7 This line is a good illustration of an "accusative of exclamation."

"Salve, puella . . ."

Catullus 43.1–4, 6–8 Modified

In this poem, Catullus shows disdain for the physical attributes of a girl whom many consider attractive or even—to his disbelief—a rival of Lesbia.

> Salvē, puella, nec minimō nāsō
> nec bellō pede nec nigrīs ocellīs
> nec longīs digitīs nec ōre siccō
> nec sānē nimis ēlegante linguā.
> 5 Tēne provincia narrat esse bellam?
> Tēcum Lesbia nostra comparātur?
> Ō saeculum insapiēns et infacētum!

ANALYSIS AND COMPREHENSION OF THE LATIN TEXT

1. What six physical features does the allegedly *bella* girl NOT possess?
2. How many "characters" are referred to in the poem?

LITERARY ANALYSIS AND DISCUSSION

1. What tone or mood is immediately established by the poet's use of the informal *salvē* rather than the more formal *avē*?
2. What is the effect of the repeated negatives (*nec . . . nec . . . nec . . . nec . . . nec . . . nec . . . nec . . .*)? **ANAPHORA** is the name given to the poetic technique that emphasizes by such repetition. Why does the negative word receive this emphasis?
3. Why do you think the poet mentions by name Lesbia but not the *puella*?
4. What is ambiguous about the poet's use of *nostra* in line 6?
5. What is highlighted by the **ANAPHORA** of *tē* in lines 5–6?
6. What insight does the poem give into what the poet finds attractive and appealing about Lesbia?

RAPID REVIEW #2: VOCATIVES AND IMPERATIVES

See Bennett, 17, 19, 25, 63, 171 and 350 and/or Gildersleeve, 23, 33, and 73 for a more detailed discussion of the vocative case. See Bennett, 281 and/or Gildersleeve, 266–275 for a more detailed discussion of the imperative mood.

VOCATIVES

1. The vocative case marks a noun and/or an adjective as being directly addressed. A noun's vocative forms tend to be the same as nominative forms, the **major** exceptions being the singular of second declension *-us* forms, *-ius* proper names and *fīlius*.

    a. for *-us* nouns and adjectives, convert the *-us* into *-e*. *Marcus>Marce, amīcus>amīce*

    b. for *-ius* proper names and *fīlius*, drop the *-us*. *Lucius>Lucī, fīlius>fīlī*

    c. **The noun *deus* lacks a vocative singular form. The adjective *meus* has *mī* for its vocative singular.**

2. A noun's vocative plural is always the same as its nominative plural.

3. A vocative form generally follows one or more words in its clause. cf. line 1 of SELECTIONS II, IV, VI and VII. But note the contrasting examples in line 4 of SELECTION VI and lines 9 and 11 in SELECTION IX.

IMPERATIVES

1. The imperative form of a verb expresses a command. Generally speaking, the singular imperative form is the same as the verb's present stem: simply remove the *-re* from the verb's present active infinitive; for the plural imperative, add *-te* to the singular. Third conjugation verbs, however, form the plural by changing the final *e>i* before adding the *-te*.

CONJUGATION	INFINITIVE	IMPERATIVES	
		SINGULAR	PLURAL
1st	portāre	port*ā*	port*āte*
2nd	docēre	doc*ē*	doc*ēte*
3rd	regere	reg*e*	reg*ite*
3rd -iō	fugere	fug*e*	fug*ite*
4th	audīre	aud*ī*	aud*īte*

2. Negative Imperatives/Prohibitions are usually expressed by a singular/plural imperative of *nōlō, nolle, nōluī* (= do not wish, be unwilling) and a complementary infinitive:

    Nōlī ambulāre in viā, mī fīlī! Do not walk in the street, my son!

    Nōlīte ambulāre in viā, meī fīliī! Do not walk in the street, my sons!

3. *NOTĀ BENE:* There are four 3rd conjugation verbs whose imperatives are irregular. Note that the plural forms of these imperatives follow the usual pattern, except for *ferte*:

	dīcere	ducere	facere	ferre
sing.	**dīc**	**duc**	**fac**	**fer**
plur.	dīcite	ducite	facite	**ferte**

PRACTICE

A. Give the vocative singular and plural for these words.

   1. agricola
   2. cīvis
   3. fīlia
   4. fīlius
   5. imperātor

   6. mīles
   7. Publius
   8. rex
   9. Rōmānus
   10. meus servus

B. Give the imperative singular and plural for these verbs.

   1. amō
   2. capiō
   3. dīcō
   4. ducō
   5. faciō

   6. ferō
   7. nōlō
   8. pōnō
   9. terreō
   10. veniō

C. Draw a circle around all vocative forms in these expressions, and <u>underline</u> all imperative forms.

   1. Simul atque tē, Lesbia, aspexī, . . .
   2. Salvē, puella, . . .
   3. Vīvāmus, mea Lesbia, atque amēmus . . .
   4. Valē, puella! . . . Scelesta, vae tē!
   5. At tū, Catulle, . . . obdūrā.
   6. Vītās mē, Chloē, . . .
   7. O dīva, . . . O rēgīna, . . . Chloēn flagellō tange . . .
   8. Tandem dēsine . . . matrem sequī . . .
   9. Ōtium, Catulle, tibi molestum est.
   10. Da mī bāsia mille!
   11. Miser Catulle, dēsinās ineptīre . . .
   12. Hīc, hīc pōnite lūcida fūnalia . . .
   13. Attice, crede mihi!
   14. Argīvās, frangite, opēs!

Catullus 86.1–6 Modified

READING VOCABULARY

Line 1 **formōsa – formōsus, -a, -um:** shapely, physically attractive/beautiful

2 **candida – candidus, -a, -um:** fair-skinned, white-complexioned

longa – longus, -a, -um: long, i.e. "tall"

recta – rectus, -a, -um: straight-backed, having a good posture/carriage

3 **singula – singulī, -ae, -a:** one-by-one, individuals

confiteor – confiteor, confitērī, confessus sum: confess, admit, acknowledge, allow, grant

4 **negō – negō, negāre, negāvī, negātum:** deny, say . . . no

nulla – nullus, -a, -um: not any, no, none

venustās – venustās, -tātis, *f.*: charm, grace, beauty, loveliness, Venus-like quality

5 **mīca salis** – a grain of salt, i.e. taste, wit

7 **sōla – sōlus, -a, -um:** alone, all by herself

surripuit – surripiō, surripere, surripuī, surreptum: steal, take away, filch

READING HELPS

Line 1–2 The contrasting datives, *multīs* and *mihi* ("to/for many," "to/for me") highlight the idea of reference and are <u>not</u> indirect objects.

3 *haec . . . singula:* neuter plurals used substantively (as nouns) as the direct object of *confiteor:* "these (things) one by one . . ."

4 *Tōtum illud:* "that totality" is used substantively as the subject of the indirect statement.

4–5 Line 5's *est* is to be inferred as the verb of line 4's *nulla venustās.*

7 *omnibus:* the idea of "separation" in the prefix of *surripuit* governs the "ablative of separation" here. *Venerēs:* "Venus-like qualities."

FYI

Line 1 It is helpful to recall that the basic idea of the dative case is "reference," i.e. the dative denotes the person(s) to whom the statement refers, of whom it is true, or to whom it is of interest. We recognize this concept most frequently in an indirect object ("He gave the gift *to me*."/"He gave *me* the gift."). The ideas of possession, separation, agency or (dis)advantage are also expressed in the dative. They are less common, to be sure, but not unusual. cf. SELECTION I, Reading Help 5.

"Quintia formosa est . . ."

Catullus 86.1–6 Modified

Catullus in this poem compares the apparently beautiful Quintia, whose charms many admire, with Lesbia. Clearly, Lesbia's qualities far outshine those of Quintia, as Catullus explores how he and others define "beauty."

> Quintia formōsa est multīs;
> mihi candida, longa, recta est:
> haec ego sīc singula confiteor.
> Tōtum illud esse formōsum negō: nam nulla venustās,
> 5   nulla mīca salis est in tam magnō corpore.
> Lesbia formōsa est, quae et pulcherrima tōta est,
> et omnibus sōla omnēs Venerēs surripuit.

ANALYSIS AND COMPREHENSION OF THE LATIN TEXT

1. The omission of conjunctions where one would normally expect to find them is another poetic technique. It is called **ASYNDETON**. Where does it occur in the opening sentence?

2. What name is given to the device exemplified in the repeated *nulla . . . nulla* in lines 4–5?

3. How many qualities of feminine beauty are mentioned in these lines? Which woman has which ones?

LITERARY ANALYSIS AND DISCUSSION

1. How does *singula* in line 3 reinforce the unconnected nature of the adjectives in line 2?

2. What does the poet gain by employing the plurals *omnēs Venerēs* (line 7)?

RAPID REVIEW #3: CORRELATIVE PAIRINGS

See Bennett, 341–344 and/or Gildersleeve, 474–497 *passim* for a more detailed discussion of this topic.

Latin employs several combinations to establish a balanced relationship within a sentence or paragraph. How many of these do you recognize?

et...et: both...and
-que...-que: both...and
neque (nec)...neque (nec): neither...nor
aut...aut: either...or
vel...vel: either...or
-ve...-ve: either...or
sīve (seu)...sīve (seu): if...or if, whether...or

nōn sōlum (modo)...sed etiam: not only...but also
tum...tum: not only...but also
ille...hic: the former...the latter
alius...alius: one...another
aliī...aliī: some...others
alter...alter: the one...the other

FYI

aut is used when the alternatives are mutually exclusive; *vel/-ve* is used to imply a choice between alternatives: *vita aut mors* vs. *aether vel caelum.*

PRACTICE

Underline the correlative combination(s) in these expressions.

1.   . . . puella nec minimō nasō
     nec bellō pede nec nigrīs ocellīs
     nec longīs digitīs nec ōre siccō
     nec sane nimis ēlegante linguā.

2.   ...quae et pulcherrima tōta est,
     et omnibus sōla omnēs Venerēs surripuit.

3.   (Catullus) nec tē requīret nec tē invītam rogābit.

4–5. Nam seu adventus vēris
      foliīs mobilibus inhorruit,
      seu viridēs lacertae rubum dīmōvērunt,
      et corde et genibus tremit.

6–9. Quis nisi vel mīles vel amāns et frīgora noctis
           et nivēs densō imbre mixtās perferet?
      Mittitur speculātor alter infestōs in hostēs,
           in rīvāle, ut hoste, alter tenet oculōs.
      Ille gravēs urbēs, hic dūrae līmen amīcae
           obsidet; hic portās frangit, at ille forēs.

10.   Hominēs multa mala aut dīcere aut facere possunt.

Catullus 5.1–13 Modified

READING VOCABULARY

Line 2 **senum – senex, (senis):** old, elderly. Used substantively, it means "old man," "codger."

        sevēriōrum – sevērus, -a, -um: stern, strict, austere

3 **assis – ās, assis,** *m.:* an as, the smallest Roman coin

        aestimēmus – aestimō, aestimāre, aestimāvī, aestimātum: value, reckon

4 **occidere – occidō, occidere, occidī, occāsum:** set, sink, fall

        resurgere – resurgō, resurgere, resurrexī, resurrectum: rise again, appear again

5 **semel –** *adv.:* once, once and for all

7 **bāsia – bāsium, bāsī,** *n.:* kiss

9 **usque –** *adv.:* all the way to

11 **conturbābimus – conturbō, conturbāre, conturbāvī, conturbātum:** thoroughly mix up, stir, confuse

12 **invidēre – invideō, invidēre, invīdī, invīsum:** be jealous of, envy, put the evil eye on, bewitch

13 **tantum – tantus, -a, -um:** so large, so great

READING HELPS

Line 1–3 The opening sentence's three verbs—*vīvāmus, amēmus* and *aestimēmus*—are examples of the hortatory/volitive usage of the subjunctive mood. Translate "let us . . "

2 Note the presence of the letter *i* in *sevēriōrum*: it signals the comparative degree.

3 *ūnīus:* The genitive case was used to express indefinite value: *Nullam togam tantī habeō* means "I have no toga of so great a value." Catullus' use of the genitive, therefore, may indicate that the *ūnīus* is less the definite idea of "one" than the indefinite idea of "an."

4 *sōlēs:* from *sōl, sōlis,* m. sun

5 *nōbīs:* dative of reference (cf. FYI in SELECTION III).

    cum: not the preposition "with" but the temporal conjunction "when."

6 What form is *dormienda*? Combining such a participle with a form of *sum* expresses obligation or necessity, something that "has to be done,""must be done" or "should be done." Here, "the night must be slept away."

7 *mī:* Do you recognize this contracted form of *mihi* from seeing it in line 1 of SELECTION I? The context (e.g. the proximity of a form of *dō*) should suggest the likelihood of a dative form rather than the vocative case of *meus* (also *mī*), seen in Rapid Review #2.

11–12 Note that the two *nē* clauses tell WHY the poet wants to "mix up" the kisses. As such, they are "adverbial purpose" subjunctive clauses.

12 Be sure to note the tricky pronoun *quis, quid*: when it occurs after *sī, nisi, nē* or *num*, it serves as a substitute for the indefinite pronoun *aliquis, aliquid*: someone/anyone, something/anything.

    malus: In poetry a commonly seen word may acquire an uncommon overtone. Here, for example, *malus* ("bad") has the overtone of "evil, mean-spirited."

13 Many readers are tempted to take the last line's *cum* as "when." Such a *"cum* circumstantial" clause, however, is usually in the imperfect or pluperfect subjunctive. No *tamen* is present, so it is unlikely that the *cum* has the concessive meaning "although." Consequently, the *cum* clause is most likely causal, "since."

FYI

Line 3   The Romans generally distinguished between definite and indefinite value by varying the case construction. The ablative case was used to express a definite price: *Togam vīgintī denariīs ēmī*, for example, means "I bought a toga for 20 *denariī*." Contrast line 3's Reading Help above.

Line 4   *Caveat lector!! Sōlēs* illustrates why precise vocabulary knowledge and a very keen eye are essential to reading Latin accurately. The fact that the ō is a long vowel means that this word is NOT a form of the verb *soleō, solēre, solitus sum* ("be accustomed"), and the fact that -*ēs* ending signals the 3ʳᵈ declension means that the word is NOT a form of *sōlus, -a, -um* ("alone, only").

Line 6   This usage of the future passive participle (also called a "gerundive") with a form of *sum* is called a "passive periphrastic." The person by whom the action "must be done" is in the dative case (dative of agent). See Major Review #2, C. 3 for more on periphrastics.

Catullus 5.1–13 Modified

This poem expresses the poet's ecstasy and delight over his first successes as he enters into his affair with Lesbia. It also addresses the *carpe diem* theme found in many poets' writings.

> **Vīvāmus, mea Lesbia, atque amēmus,**
> **rūmōrēsque omnēs senum sevēriōrum**
> **ūnīus assis aestimēmus!**
> **Sōlēs occidere et resurgere possunt:**
> 5 **nōbīs cum semel brevis lux occidit,**
> **nox perpetua ūna dormienda est.**
> **Da mī bāsia mille, deinde centum;**
> **deinde mille altera, deinde secunda centum;**
> **deinde usque altera mille, deinde centum.**
> 10 **Deinde, cum mīlia multa fēcerīmus,**
> **conturbābimus illa, nē sciāmus,**
> **aut nē quis malus invidēre possit**
> **cum sciat tantum esse numerum bāsiōrum.**

ANALYSIS AND COMPREHENSION OF THE LATIN TEXT

1. Note the progression from the more formally polite "hortatory" subjunctives in lines 1–3 to the direct imperative in line 7. What is the reason, given in lines 4–6, for the greater directness and urgency of line 7?

2. The poetic device of **METAPHOR** is a form of comparison, using a word or phrase to imply a likeness between what is described and something else. What **METAPHORS** are found in lines 4–6?

3. What two specific reasons does Catullus give for "mixing up" all the kisses? How could each reason have endangered the outpouring of kisses?

4. Two more poetic devices: **ALLITERATION** is the repetition of the same initial sound, usually a consonant, in two or more words, while **ASSONANCE** is the close repetition of similar sounds and is usually applied to vowels. **HYPERBOLE** was defined earlier (SELECTION I). What examples of these three devices appear in this selection?

Cupid and Psyche kissing

LITERARY ANALYSIS AND DISCUSSION

1. What is the dramatic effect of the three subjunctive mood verbs in the poem's opening sentence?

2. Why might *sōlēs* be plural but *lux* singular?

RAPID REVIEW #4: FORMATION OF THE PRESENT SUBJUNCTIVE

1st conjugation verbs: sign of a present subjunctive is an *-ē*. 2nd, 3rd, 3rd *-iō* and 4th conjugation verbs: sign of a present subjunctive is an *-ā*. To remember more easily the vowel markers of the present subjunctive, it may be useful to learn the following memnonic: Sh**e** w**ea**rs **a** di**a**mond. The active voice has been conjugated below as an example:

		SHE	WEARS	A	DIAMOND	
		1st Conjugation	2nd Conjugation	3rd Conjugation	3rd-io Conjugation	4th Conjugation
Sing.	1	port*em*	doc*eam*	reg*am*	fug*iam*	aud*iam*
	2	port*ēs*	doc*eās*	reg*ās*	fug*iās*	aud*iās*
	3	port*et*	doc*eat*	reg*at*	fug*iat*	aud*iat*
Plur.	1	port*ēmus*	doc*eāmus*	reg*āmus*	fug*iāmus*	aud*iāmus*
	2	port*ētis*	doc*eātis*	reg*ātis*	fug*iātis*	aud*iātis*
	3	port*ent*	doc*eant*	reg*ant*	fug*iant*	aud*iant*

		esse
Sing.	1	sim
	2	sīs
	3	sit
Plur.	1	sīmus
	2	sītis
	3	sint

<u>So also</u>: **velim, nōlim, mālim, possim,** and other compounds of **sum**

ire
eam
eās
eat
eāmus
eātis
eant

<u>So also</u>: **feram, fīam**

PRACTICE

You will remember that there is no set meaning for a subjunctive verb in Latin, but that the subjunctive verb's usage (construction in which it occurs) determines the meaning. A reader's ability to recognize quickly and correctly a verb form's "mood" (indicative/subjunctive) is vital. This drill will help you gauge <u>your</u> ability.

Determine the person, number, tense, voice and mood for these verb forms.

1. amātur	6. cupient	11. fit	16. eāmus	21. sciēmur
2. timēs	7. scīmur	12. fīat	17. iimus	22. cupiant
3. mittō	8. sciāmur	13. fertis	18. ferētis	23. mittam (indic.)
4. mittam (subj.)	9. possītis	14. ferātis	19. fīet	24. timeās
5. cupiunt	10. possētis	15. īmus	20. potestis	25. amētur

Catullus 70.1–4 Modified

READING VOCABULARY

Line 1 **nūbere – nūbō, nūbere, nupsī, nuptum:** wed, marry (+ dat.)

malle – mālō, malle, māluī, _____: wish more, prefer (+ complementary infinitive)

3 **cupidō – cupidus, -a, -um:** desirous, eager

amantī – amāns, -ntis, *m.:* a lover

ventō – ventus, -ī, *m.:* wind, breeze

4 **oportet –** from the impersonal verb *oportet, oportēre, oportuit:* it is proper, it is right, it is necessary; one should

READING HELPS

Line 1 Remember that in indirect discourse—statement, command or question—a reflexive pronoun like *sē* has the main verb's subject as its antecedent. Consequently, the antecedent for *sē* here is *mulier.* See Major Review #1, III for more information on Indirect Statement.

nullī quam mihi is a tricky phrase, for there is a *magis* (comparative adverb: more) implied in *malle* (= *magis velle*) that accounts for the *quam* meaning "than:" " no one more than (before) me."

2 *petat:* The present subjunctive form signifies an "ideal" (or "future less vivid") conditional clause. Translate "should seek." One needs to pay especially close attention to the tense and mood of a subjunctive verb in conditional clauses. Rapid Review #9 goes into the topic of conditional sentences in more detail.

3 Note that the relative pronoun *quod* has an implied *id* as an antecedent: "that which." cf. SELECTION I, Reading Help 5.

4 Instead of having a personal subject such as "I" or "they," an impersonal verb has an infinitive, a clause or a neuter pronoun for its subject. The English "It's raining!" and "It's nice to see you!" and "To err is human!" are typical examples. The infinitive *scrībere* is the subject of *oportet,* defining what "is necessary."

Catullus 70.1–4 Modified

In this poem, Catullus expresses his frustration at the discrepancy between Lesbia's words and her actions. Some scholars consider this poem to be among the first in a series of poems in which Catullus attempts to analyze the failure of his relationship with Lesbia.

> **Mulier mea dīcit sē nullī quam mihi nūbere malle,**
> **nōn sī Iuppiter ipse sē petat.**
> **Dīcit: sed quod mulier cupidō amantī dīcit**
> **in ventō et rapidā aquā scrībere oportet.**

ANALYSIS AND COMPREHENSION OF THE LATIN TEXT

1. Are there examples of **ANAPHORA** (repetition) in the poem?

LITERARY ANALYSIS AND DISCUSSION

1. **IRONY** is a device by which one mentions a supposed fact with the clear intent of implying its opposite. It may express humor, ridicule, or light sarcasm. Is there any irony in this poem? Support your response, if it is affirmative, with specific reference(s) to the Latin text.

2. Why are **ANAPHORA** and **HYPERBOLE** effective devices for this poem?

Jupiter

RAPID REVIEW #5: FIVE USES OF *QUAM*

1. Relative pronoun: accusative, singular, feminine—means "whom," "which" or "that," NOT "what"

   Example: *Puella quam vīdī fuit pulchra.*
                   The girl whom (or that) I saw was pretty.

2. Interrogative adjective: accusative, singular, feminine—means "which" or "what," NOT "whom"

   Example: *Quam puellam pulchram vīdistī?*
                   What/Which pretty girl did you see?

3. Before a positive degree adjective or adverb—means "how"

   Example: *Quam ferus est ille canis!*
                   How fierce that dog is!

4. After a comparative degree adjective or adverb—means "than"

   Example: *Meus canis est ferior quam tuus.*
                   My dog is fiercer than yours.

5. Before a superlative degree adjective or adverb—means "as _____ as possible"

   Example: *Canis noster est quam ferissimus.*
                   Our dog is as fierce as possible.

In a sentence like #4, when the two being compared are <u>nominative</u> or <u>accusative</u> case, it is permissible to substitute an "ablative of comparison" for the *"quam* + the same case" construction. Consequently, #4 could also correctly be written: *Meus canis est ferior tuō.*

PRACTICE

Translate, paying special attention to the uses of *quam*.

1. Quam formōsa fuit Lesbia!
2. Maria est pulchrior quam Quintia, sed Lesbia est pulcherrima omnium trium.
3. Lucius nōn est celerior Marcō, sed est quam fortissimus!
4. Quam puellam Catullus amāvit?
5. Puella quam Catullus amāvit Lesbia fuit.

Catullus 8.12–19 Modified

READING VOCABULARY

Line 1 **obdūrat – obdūrō, obdūrāre, obdūrāvī, obdūr-ātum:** be hard against, stand out, persist, be firm, be tough

2 **requīret – re+quaerō>requīrō, requīrere, requīsīvī, requīsītum:** ask back, seek again

invītam – invītus, -a, -um: unwilling, against one's will

3 **at –** *conj.:* but

dolēbis – doleō, dolēre, doluī, dolitum: suffer grief, pain or hurt

4 **scelesta – scelestus, -a, -um:** wicked, evil, accursed, infamous

vae – *interjection:* woe! damn!

5 **adībit – adeō, adīre, adiī, aditum:** go to, approach, visit

7 **bāsiābis – bāsiō, bāsiāre, bāsiāvī, bāsiātum:** kiss

labella – labellum, -ī, *n.:* the diminuitive of *labrum:* little lip

mordēbis – mordeō, mordēre, momordī, morsum: bite, nip, nibble on

8 **destinātus – destinātus, -a, -um:** stubborn, fixed, determined, settled, having made up one's mind

READING HELPS

Line 1–7 Pay close attention to verb tenses, for the poet switches back and forth from present to future.

3 *at* is a very strongly emotional or emphatic word of contrast—"BUT."

cum: The lack of a word in the ablative case after *cum* indicates that it is a temporal conjunction, not a preposition.

nihil—used adverbially here: "not at all."

4 *vae* is an emphatic interjection expressing pain, disgust or anger, almost a curse, and takes the dative or accusative.

Quae is the first of a series of seven interrogative pronoun or adjective forms. You may want to review the forms and meanings for the interrogative pronoun *quis quid* vs. the interrogative adjective *quī quae quod.*

Tibi is a dative of reference. cf. SELECTION I, Reading Help 5 or SELECTION III, Reading Help 1–2 and FYI.

5 *vidēberis:* if this word causes trouble, review SELECTION I, Reading Help 1 about the meaning of the passive voice of *video.*

Orpheus/Eurydice

Catullus 8.12–19 Modified

The text of this selection constitutes the closing lines of a poem in which Catullus rationally understands that his relationship with Lesbia is over, but emotionally is reluctant to admit its demise. Here, although Catullus tries to brace himself for the toughness needed to say "farewell," to some readers his storm of passionate questions sweeps aside his avowed resolve.

> Valē, puella! Iam Catullus obdūrat,
> nec tē requīret nec tē invītam rogābit.
> At tū dolēbis, cum nihil rogāberis.
> Scelesta, vae tē! Quae vīta tibi manet?
> 5   Quis tē nunc adībit? Cui bella vidēberis?
> Quem nunc amābis? Cūius esse dīcēris?
> Quem bāsiābis? Cūius labella mordēbis?
> At tū, Catulle, destinātus obdūrā.

ANALYSIS AND COMPREHENSION OF THE LATIN TEXT

1. What decision does Catullus seem to have made? What does he say its effect will be on the *puella*?
2. What is the impact of *tū* in line 3? Consider how Latin uses the nominative case of the personal pronouns.
3. Which of the seven interrogative forms in these lines are interrogative pronouns?
4. How many questions are piled up in lines 4–7? What kind of questions are they: factual? deliberative? rhetorical?
5. What kind of word is the initial *valē?* the final *obdūrā?*

LITERARY ANALYSIS AND DISCUSSION

1. *vae* is a strongly emotional word. What is a modern equivalent for expressing such a hope that someone will suffer woe or damnation?
2. What is the effect of all the piled up questions in lines 4–7?
3. These lines are filled with emotions, mood swings and contrasts. What causes them?
4. Is *destinātus* an accurate description of Catullus?

RAPID REVIEW #6: INTERROGATIVE PRONOUNS AND ADJECTIVES

See Bennett, 90, 162 ff. or Gildersleeve, 106, 450–470 for a detailed discussion of interrogative pronouns and adjectives.

INTERROGATIVE PRONOUNS AND ADJECTIVES

1. A pronoun introducing a question is called an interrogative pronoun. Since it introduces a question, it has NO antecedent. *quis? quid?* **"who?" "what?" (NOT "which?")**

    Example: *Quis venit? Quid portat?*
                 Who is coming? What is he carrying?

2. An adjective introducing a question is called an interrogative adjective and, like any adjective, must agree with its modified noun in case, number and gender. *quī? quae? quod?* **"which?" "what?" (NOT who?)**

    Example: *Quī puer venit? Quam puellam vidēs? Quod tēlum mīles portat?*
                 What boy is coming? Which girl do you see?
                 What spear is the soldier carrying?

3. In the "ablative of accompaniment" usage of an interrogative pronoun (but not adjective), the *cum* is attached as an enclitic (as is the case with personal, relative and reflexive pronouns).

    Examples: Interrogative Pron.   *Quōcum/Quibuscum herī ambulābātis?*
                                          With whom were you walking yesterday?

                  Personal Pron.   *Mēcum/tēcum/nōbīscum/vōbīscum vēnit.*
                                          He came with me/with you/with us/with you (pl.).

                  Relative Pron.   *Puer quōcum ambulat meus frāter est.*
                                          The boy with whom he is walking is my brother.

                  Reflexive Pron.   *Puer dīxit puellam sēcum vēnisse.*
                                          The boy said that the girl had come with him.

                  Interrogative Adj.   *Cum quibus amīcīs ad forum vēnistī?*
                                          With what friends did you come to the forum?

PRACTICE

A. **Translate the following short contextual drills.**

1. Quae mulier mea dīcit?
2. Quis mihi nūbere mavult?
3. Quid mulier mea dīxit?
4. Quī malī invidēre possunt?
5. Cuius verba in ventō scrībī dēbent?

6. Cum quārum digitīs digitī Lesbiae comparantur?
7. Quibuscum Lesbia mea comparātur?
8. Ā quō illa puella esse bella narrātur?
9. Cum quibus puellīs Lesbia mea comparātur?
10. Quibus in provinciā haec narrantur? Cui puella mea haec dīxit?

B. **Indicate whether the italicized expression contains an interrogative adjective (IA) or pronoun (IP). Then try to put the expression into correct Latin. There may be more than one correct way to do so.**

1. *Whom* does she love?
2. *What* are important to a lover?
3. *With whom* is she speaking?
4. *With what* was he compared?
5. *By whose friend* is she compared to Lesbia?

6. *To what girl* did he give a gift?
7. *In what country* is Verona?
8. *Whose* friend is she?
9. *To whom* are these things told?
10. *To whom* will the lover flee?

MAJOR REVIEW #1

INFINITIVE FORMATION, LITERAL TRANSLATION AND BASIC USAGES

See Bennett, 270 and 326–335 or Gildersleeve, 112 ff., 419–434 for a more detailed discussion of this topic.

I. DEFINITION, FORMATION AND LITERAL TRANSLATION

An **infinitive** is a verb form not limited (*in finītus*—not bounded) by person or number though it does have tense and voice.

Latin has five infinitive forms that commonly occur.

	ACTIVE FORM	ACTIVE MEANING	PASSIVE FORM	PASSIVE MEANING
PRESENT	2nd principal part --------------------- docēre regere	to _____ --------------------- to teach to rule	1st, 2nd, and 4th: *-re* inf. ending becomes *-rī* 3rd and 3rd-*io*: *-ere* inf. ending becomes *-ī* --------------------- docērī regī	to be ___ed --------------------- to be taught to be ruled
PERFECT	3rd principal part stem + *-isse* --------------------- docuisse rexisse	to have ___ed --------------------- to have taught to have ruled	4th principal part stem + *-us -a -um esse* --------------------- doctus, -a, -um esse rectus, -a, -um esse	to have been ___ed --------------------- to have been taught to have been ruled
FUTURE	4th principal part stem + *-ūrus -a -um esse* --------------------- doctūrus, -a, -um esse rectūrus, -a, -um esse	to be about (going) to ___ --------------------- to be about to teach to be about to rule	THIS FORM IS VERY RARE.	

DRILL

A. Form AND translate literally the infinitives of these verbs (all seen in SELECTIONS I–VI):

   1. bāsiō   2. mordeō   3. tegō   4. surripiō   5. audiō

B. Identify the form (tense and voice) and literally translate these infinitives.

1. amāre	6. scīrī	11. amārī	16. cēpisse	21. amātum esse
2. monērī	7. captūrum esse	12. monuisse	17. monēre	22. monitūrus esse
3. dīxisse	8. dīcere	13. dictūra esse	18. scīre	23. dīcī
4. captus esse	9. monita esse	14. capere	19. amātūra esse	24. capī
5. scītūrus esse	10. amāvisse	15. scītum esse	20. dictus esse	25. scīvisse

II. BASIC USAGES

Though an infinitive is a verb form, it also has the noun characteristics of gender (neuter) and number (singular). When an infinitive occurs in a phrase rather than by itself, its subject is in the **accusative** case:

Infinitive by itself: Puella <u>discēdere</u> cupit. The girl desires <u>to leave</u>.

Infinitive in phrase: Puella <u>puerum discēdere</u> cupit. The girl desires <u>the boy to leave</u>.

Note that this is similar to English usage where an infinitive's subject is in the objective form, not the nominative: He wants <u>us</u> (not "we") to depart. **Remember: infinitives are neuter and their subjects are accusative.** Though Latin uses infinitives, alone or in phrases, in at least eight different ways, three are really quite uncommon, and assistance will be provided, should one be met in a reading. Here are the five commonly encountered uses. They are essential and should be mastered!

1. SUBJECT: *<u>Errāre</u> est humānum!* (Explain the ending on *humānum*).

2. PREDICATE NOUN: *Vidēre est <u>crēdere</u>.* (What is the subject?)

3. DIRECT OBJECT: *Cupisne <u>lūdere</u>? <u>Puerōs discēdere</u> iussit.* (What case is *puerōs*? Why?)

4. COMPLEMENTARY: Several verbs take an infinitive to fill out **(complement)** their meaning. Among the most common are:

   audeō, audēre, ausus sum: dare (to)
   constituō, constituere, constituī, constitūtum: decide (to), determine (to)
   dēbeō, dēbēre, dēbuī, dēbitum: ought (to)
   possum, posse, potuī, _____: be able (to), can
   soleō, solēre, solitus sum: be accustomed (to)
   temptō, 1 and conor, conārī, conātus sum: try (to), attempt (to)
   videor, vidērī, vīsus sum: seem (to), seem best (to)
   volō/nōlō/mālō: be willing (to)/unwilling (to)/prefer (to)

   N.B.   The English expressions "could have . . ." and "should have . . ." or "ought to have . . ." are expressed by a **past** time form of *possum* or *dēbeō* with a **present** infinitive.

5. VERB OF INDIRECT STATEMENT: This major subject will be taken up in section III (below the **DRILL**).

DRILL

Identify each infinitive's form (tense and voice) and usage.

1. Puellae bonae laudārī dēbent.
2. Mea mulier mī nūbere māvult.
3. Dīcere est facile, difficile agere.
4. Sōlēs occidere et resurgere possunt.
5. Ea suam fīliam ab omnibus puerīs spectārī nōn cupīvit.
6. Pater māterque suōs fīliōs esse sānōs cupiunt.
7. Amīcum dēcipere turpe est.
8. Puer malus illud facere nōn dēbuit.
9. Ille mī pār esse deō vidētur.
10. Difficile est longum subitō dēpōnere amōrem.

III. INDIRECT STATEMENT

See Bennett, 314 ff. or Gildersleeve, 112 ff., 527 ff. for a more detailed discussion of this topic.

A. In order to grasp the essentials of <u>indirect</u> statement, one must understand <u>direct</u> statement. Study these three sentences:

1. These books are good.
   Hī librī sunt bonī.

   An **Independent Clause** serving as a declarative sentence.

2. The teacher says, "These books are good."
   Magister "Hī librī" inquit "sunt bonī."

   A **Direct** Statement/Quotation of the sentence.

3. The teacher said that these books were good.
   Magister dixit hōs librōs esse bonōs.

   An **Indirect** Statement relaying the gist of the sentence but not using exactly the same words.

B. Pay close attention to the following points:

1. A **direct** statement is an independent clause (#1 above) in quotation marks (#2 above).

2. An <u>English</u> **indirect** statement (#3 above) is:

   a. a clause dependent on a sensory verb—one involving actions of the head, like seeing, hearing, thinking, saying, feeling, perceiving, believing, etc.

   b. introduced by the subordinating conjunction "that"

   c. lacking quotation marks.

3. A <u>Latin</u> indirect statement (#3 above) does NOT use a subordinating conjunction for the "that"; instead it expresses the verb of the indirect statement ("were") as an infinitive rather than a regular verb form. Because the verb of the Latin indirect statement is an infinitive, the subject of the indirect statement ("these books") is in the accusative case. Because "were" is a linking verb with a predicate adjective describing the subject ("books"), "good" is masculine accusative plural *bonōs* to agree with *librōs*.

C. A final caution: a reflexive pronoun or reflexive possessive adjective in an indirect statement refers to the main verb's nominative subject, NOT the indirect statement's accusative subject. *Pater audīvit puerum fīliam <u>suam</u> amāre.* The father heard that the boy was in love with <u>his</u> (the father's) daughter.

D. Tenses of the infinitive in indirect statement.

1. The tense of the infinitive in indirect statement is not absolute but always is relative (shows a relationship) to the time of the introductory main verb:

   a. a present infinitive means that its action happens at the same time as the main verb's action: time contemporaneous.

   b. a perfect infinitive means that its action happened before the main verb's action: time prior.

   c. a future infinitive means that its action will happen after the main verb's action: time subsequent.

2. This concept—generally a puzzling subject when first encountered—can be understood by pondering the following examples. Once it is understood, a shorthand solution is to apply the "magic formula" found in section E.

3.   Examples:

    a. NON-PAST TIME MAIN VERB + PRESENT INFIN.   TRANSLATION

        Dīcit (Dīcet, Dixerit) puerum aquam portāre.   He says (will say, will have said) that the boy **is** carrying the water.

        Dīcit (Dīcet, Dixerit) aquam ā puerō portārī.   He says (will say, will have said) that water **is being** carried by a boy.

    b. NON-PAST TIME MAIN VERB + PERFECT INFIN.   TRANSLATION

        Dīcit (Dīcet, Dixerit) puerum aquam portāvisse.   He says (will say, will have said) that the boy **has** carried the water.

        Dīcit (Dīcet, Dixerit) aquam ā puerō portātam esse.   He says (will say, will have said) that water **has been** carried by a boy.

    c. NON-PAST TIME MAIN VERB + FUTURE INFIN.   TRANSLATION

        Dīcit (Dīcet, Dixerit) puerum aquam portātūrum esse.   He says (will say, will have said) that the boy **will** (**is going to**) carry the water.

---

    d. PAST TIME MAIN VERB + PRESENT INFIN.   TRANSLATION

        Dixit (Dixerat, Dīcēbat) puerum aquam portāre.   He said (had said, was saying) that the boy **was** carrying the water.

        Dixit (Dixerat, Dīcēbat) aquam ā puerō portārī.   He said (had said, was saying) that water **was being** carried by a boy.

    e. PAST TIME MAIN VERB + PERFECT INFIN.   TRANSLATION

        Dixit (Dixerat, Dīcēbat) puerum aquam portāvisse.   He said (had said, was saying) that the boy **had** carried the water.

        Dixit (Dixerat, Dīcēbat) aquam ā puerō portātam esse.   He said (had said, was saying) that water **had been** carried by a boy.

    f. PAST TIME MAIN VERB + FUTURE INFIN.   TRANSLATION

        Dixit (Dixerat, Dīcēbat) puerum aquam portātūrum esse.   He said (had said, was saying) that the boy **would** (**was going to**) carry the water.

E. "MAGIC FORMULA."

Non-Past Time Main Verb (present, future, fut. perf.)	Ind. State. Infinitive	Translation	
	pres. act.	is (are) ____ing	IS
	pres. pass.	is (are) being ____d	
	perf. act.	have (has) ____d	HAS
	perf. pass.	have (has) been ____d	
	fut. act.	will (is/are going to) ____	WILL

Past Time Main Verb (imperf., perfect, pluperf.)	Ind. State. Infinitive	Translation	
	pres. act.	was (were) ____ing	WAS
	pres. pass.	was (were) being ____d	
	perf. act.	had ____d	HAD
	perf. pass.	had been ____d	
	fut. act.	would (was/were going to) ____	WOULD

DRILL A

Translate these contextual sentences, using the "magic formula."

1. Catullus (hodiē) dīcit sē Lesbiam (hodiē) amāre.
2. Catullus (hodiē) dīcit sē Lesbiam (herī) amāvisse.
3. Catullus (hodiē) dīcit sē Lesbiam (crās) amātūrum esse.
4. Catullus (hodiē) dīcit Lesbiam ā sē (hodiē) amārī.
5. Catullus (hodiē) dīcit Lesbiam ā sē (herī) amātam esse.
6. Poēta (herī) scrīpsit sē Lesbiam (herī) amāre.
7. Poēta (herī) scrīpsit sē Lesbiam (prīdiē) amāvisse.
8. Poēta (herī) scrīpsit sē Lesbiam (hodiē, crās, semper) amātūrum esse.
9. Poēta (herī) scrīpsit Lesbiam ā sē (herī) amārī.
10. Poēta (herī) scrīpsit Lesbiam ā sē (prīdiē) amātam esse.

These sentences are based upon Catullan poems not included in this *Libellus:* translate.

11. Cornēlius putābat meās nūgās esse aliquid. (**Cornelius** was the person to whom Catullus dedicated his collection of poems. *nūgae:* "triflings, scribblings." *aliquis, aliquid:* "someone, something" here.)
12. Catullus putāvit mīlia versuum ā Suffēnō perscrīpta esse. (**Suffenus** was an aspiring poet whom Catullus did not appreciate, for S. equated quantity with quality. *versus,-ūs, m.:* "verse, line of verse." The prefix *per-* adds intensity to a word: *thoroughly, completely, exceedingly, very much:* here, perhaps: "written to excess.")
13. Mea puella vōvit sē ēlectissima pessimī poētae scrīpta tardipedī deō datūram esse. (*voveō, vovēre, vōvī, vōtum:* "promise, vow"; *ēlectissimus, -a, um:* "choicest, most select": *tardipēs deus* is a humorous way to refer to the lame Vulcan, god of fire.)
14. Prōvinciane narrābat amīcam Formiānī esse bellam? (The *prōvincia* is personified and contrasts with the taste of the *urbs*, Rome. *Formiānus:* "the Formian"; Mamurra from Formiae was a wealthy associate of Julius Caesar and much disliked by Catullus.)

15. Lesbia quondam dīcēbat sē sōlum Catullum amāvisse. (*quondam:* "formerly, once upon a time"; *sōlus, -a, -um:* "alone, only.")

16. Catullus cōgitāvit sē esse pium neque sanctam fīdem violāvisse. (*pius, -a, -um:* "dutiful, loyal, true"; *fidēs, -ēī, f.:* "vow, promise, trust.")

17. Nulla mulier vērē dīcere potest sē tantum amātam esse quantum Lesbiam meam ā mē amātam esse. (*vērē:* "truly"; *tantum . . . quantum:* "as much . . . as . . .")

18. Prōpōnis mihi, mea Lesbia, hunc amōrem nostrum inter nōs perpetuumque fore. (*prōpōnō:* "propose, offer"; *fore* = **futūrum** *esse*.)

19. Catullus cōgitāvit poēma ā Caeciliō venustē incohātum esse. (*poēma, -atis, n.:* "poem"; **Caecilius** was a love-poet from Como, near Catullus' home town of Verona; *venustē incohātum esse:* "charmingly begun.")

20. Poēta dīxit frātrem Polliōnis manū sinistrā nōn bellē ūsum esse. (**Pollio** was a distinguished Roman, an associate of Julius Caesar, and close friend of the poets Horace and Vergil. He founded Rome's first public library. *Ūtor, ūtī, ūsus sum:* "take advantage of, use" [+ abl.].)

DRILL B (AND REVIEW)

Reread the following sentences (or parts of sentences); then identify each infinitive's form and usage.

SELELCTION I:	lines 1–2:	Ille mī par esse deō vidētur, ille, sī fas est, mī superāre dīvōs vidētur, . . .
SELECTION II:	line 5:	Tēne provincia narrat esse bellam?
SELECTION III:	line 4:	Tōtum illud esse formōsum negō: . . .
SELECTION IV:	line 4:	Sōlēs occidere et resurgere possunt: . . .
	lines 10–13:	Deinde, cum mīlia multa fēcerīmus, conturbābimus illa, nē sciāmus, aut nē quis malus invidēre possit cum sciat tantum esse numerum basiōrum.
SELECTION V:	all:	Mulier mea dīcit sē nullī quam mihi nūbere malle, nōn sī Iuppiter ipse sē petat. Dīcit: sed quod mulier cupidō amantī dīcit in ventō et rapidā aquā scrībere oportet.

It is hard to envision two poets more unlike in their backgrounds than Catullus and Horace. Tradition holds that Catullus was from a prosperous and influential family in Verona in Cisalpine Gaul to the north of Rome. Horace, about twenty years younger, supposedly was the son of an ex-slave, a freedman in Venusia, which was a small town in impoverished lower Italy. Horace's father seems to have been wealthy enough, however, to provide his son with top-notch educational opportunities. That meant bringing young Horace to Rome rather than schooling him in Venusia. Both Catullus and Horace, therefore, were in Rome during tumultuous times socially and politically (cf. **Introduction to Catullus**).

Details about Horace's life are scattered throughout his *Satires* and *Epistles*, and a short *vīta* survives, probably written by the first century biographer Suetonius. Not much is known, however, about the reliability of these sources. The poet reportedly was born Quintus Horatius Flaccus in early December of 65 BCE. Though nothing is known of his mother, his father seems to have been an auctioneer or perhaps a tax collector or maybe a dealer of salted fish. The evidence is not clear. His father recognized Horace's talent and determined to foster it to the very best of his ability. That meant schooling in Rome, preferably with a noted teacher. His *grammaticus* Orbilius apparently practiced stern discipline: in his *Epistles*, Horace describes him as *plagōsus* (fond of flogging). Horace's father too kept a close eye on his son, for Horace relates that his father (rather than a *paedagōgus*) walked with him to and from school, carefully supervised his studies and play, and did his best to instill sound character and morals. In later years the poet wrote a touching, appreciative acknowledgement to this "best of fathers."

After Horace had completed his introductory studies of grammar and poetry (the basics of lower education at that time), he probably studied rhetoric with a second teacher. When he was about nineteen or twenty, he went to Athens for advanced study of philosophy and poetry (the equivalent of a university education). He seems to have been particularly interested in the philosophy of Epicurus and, like Catullus and his friends, in the early Greek lyric poetry of Alcaeus and Sappho. He also seems to have associated with a group of well-born young Romans there, among them the young Cicero, son of the famous politician, and M. Valerius Messalla, later one of the distinguished orators of the age.

While Horace was studying in Athens, events were in a turmoil back in Rome, and ultimately the dictator Julius Caesar was assassinated. Amid all the political and social upheavals, M. Junius Brutus, one of the plotters, arrived in Greece, championing the side of the "loyal opposition." Horace writes that he joined this republican side of the struggle. Despite a lack of any previous military training or experience, he was appointed a *tribūnus mīlitum* in the army of Brutus and Cassius. The forces of Antony and Octavian routed the republican army at Philippi in October, 42 BCE. The poet writes that he fought "not well" in this battle and found himself in difficulty afterwards. His father had died, and his inheritance was taken by the victorious Octavian because Horace had supported the losing republican side.

After a general amnesty was granted to the losers, Horace returned to Rome (41 BCE) and apparently obtained a position as *scrība quaestorius*, a secretary in the treasury office. This post provided enough financial security to enable a return to writing poetry, and he seems to have soon become a close friend of two other rising young poets, Varius and Vergil. Through them, in 39 BCE, he came to the attention of Maecenas. He was an influential advisor to Octavian, particularly in matters of culture and public imagery. From Maecenas Horace relates that he received his Sabine farm, located about thirty miles from Rome. This farm provided to the poet not only economic stability but also a favorite spot for inspiration and relaxation. Through his relationship with Maecenas, Horace soon began mingling with the very highest levels of Roman society. He became close friends with leading politicians like Pollio and Agrippa and with cultural shining lights like Quintilius Varus, Aristius Fuscus and the poet Tibullus. These friends' names are scattered throughout his poems.

Octavian/Augustus Caesar

Through Maecenas, too, Horace became a cordial and close companion of Octavian, better known as the emperor Augustus. Even though as a youth he opposed Octavian, the more mature Horace seems to have recognized the potential for steadiness and effective government under the new regime, and he supported it with his artistic talents. The *vīta* (cf. paragraph 2) of Horace reports that Augustus offered him a position as his private secretary; the fact that Horace felt free to decline the offer may say a great deal about what close friends they were. That the emperor commissioned Horace to write the *Carmen Saeculāre* testifies to his role as poet laureate.

Like Catullus, Horace valued Callimachean brevity and wit in his poetry (cf. Introduction to Catullus). He adopted the *persōna* (mask) of a rather mellow, experienced, philosophical world traveler who had seen, enjoyed and learned much. Many of his poems have an addressee, either a real or an imaginary person. The poet muses philosophically on politics, love, life, death, literature and much more. Horace remains much admired for his clever turns of phrase, for his genial humor, for his sense of the ironic and paradoxical, and for his artful arrangement of words and structure within a poem. His language, unlike Catullus' spicy colloquialism, is more refined, polite and formal. Horace is famous for his flexible word order, and he uses adjectives to add color or particularizing detail. Within a poem an adjective is often quite far removed from the noun it describes. These forceful separations (the technique is called **HYPERBATON**) often create unexpected as-

sociations, contrasts, humor or emphasis. Horace draws much of his imagery from nature. He is fond of citing examples, often from mythology, to highlight or "prove" the point of a poem. Thematic words or ideas are located at the beginning of a poem or of a line. Transitions within a poem often occur near its structural midpoint, and a poem often winds down to a quiet close, with concluding vocabulary or ideas that recall the poem's beginning.

Horace, Vergil, Varus and Maecenas

Horace is reported to have died in the autumn of 8 BCE, just before his fifty-seventh birthday and just a few weeks after his friend Maecenas had also died. Besides the *Carmen Saeculāre*, he left us his *Epodēs*, two books of *Sermōnēs* (or *Satires*), four books of *Odes*, and two books of *Epistulae*. Selections VII–IX come from his *Odes*, published in the late 20s BCE.

TIMELINE FOR HORACE

? 65 BCE ?	H. born
? 46/45 BCE ?	H. to Greece
42 BCE	Philippi
41 BCE	H. to Rome
39 BCE	H. introduced to Maecenas
33 BCE	H. gets farm
23 BCE	*Odes* I–III published
? 8 BCE ?	H. dies

Horace

Horace *Odes* I.23.1–12 Modified

READING VOCABULARY

Line 1 **vītās** – **vītō, vītāre, vītāvī, vītātum:** avoid, shun

inuleō – **inuleus, -ī,** *m.:* a fawn, young deer

Chloē – **Chloē, Chloes,** *f.:* a woman's name. The Greek word *chloē* means "green bud, twig, shoot."

2 **pavidam** – **pavidus, -a, -um:** quaking, trembling (with fear)

3 **āviīs** – **āvius, -a, -um:** pathless, trackless, remote

4 **metū** – **metus, -ūs,** *m.:* fear, dread

aurārum – **aura, -ae,** *f.:* breeze

5 **adventus** – **adventus, -ūs,** *m.:* arrival, approach

vēris – **vēr, vēris,** *n.:* spring (season)

6 **foliīs** – **folium, -ī,** *n.:* leaf, foliage

mobilibus – **mobilis, -e:** mobile, movable; nimble, active; shifty, changing

inhorruit – **inhorrescō, inhorrescere, inhorruī, _____:** begin to tremble, quiver, shake; i.e. rustle, make a rustling sound; begin to bristle, stand on end (i.e. become stiff or erect)

7 **viridēs** – **viridis, -e:** green, fresh, young, lively, vigorous

lacertae – **lacerta, -ae,** *f.:* a lizard

rubum – **rubus, -ī,** *m.:* a bramble-bush, blackberry

8 **corde** – **cor, cordis,** *n.:* heart

genibus – **genū, -ūs,** *n.:* knee

tremit – **tremō, tremere, tremuī, _____:** tremble, shiver, quake

9 **atquī** – (like *at*, seen earlier, this is a very strong adversative word): AND YET, BUT

frangere – **frangō, frangere, frēgī, fractum:** break, crush, maul

persequor – **persequor, persequī, persecūtus sum:** hunt, pursue, track, punish, avenge

10 **ut** – *introducing a simile:* as

aspera – **asper, -era, -erum:** fierce, rough, wild, harsh, cruel

Gaetūlus – **Gaetūlus, -a, -um:** Gaetulian. Gaetulia was an area in northwestern Africa renowned for its lions.

-ve – *enclitic* (like *-que*): or

11 **tandem** – an adverb expressing considerable impatience: finally, at last; once and for all

dēsine – **dēsinō, dēsinere, dēsiī, dēsitum:** stop, halt, cease (+ complementary infinitive)

tempestīva – **tempestīvus, -a, -um:** seasonable, fit, ripe, timely, mature (+ dative)

READING HELPS

Line 1 *Similis* is one of the adjectives that takes the dative case.

2 *quaerentī* is a present active participle that modifies *inuleō* and takes *mātrem* as its object.

7 The *dī-* prefix on *dīmōvērunt* adds the idea of "apart, in different directions."

8 The subject of *tremit* is generally considered to be the fawn, though it can be the fawn's mother.

9 The infinitive *frangere* expresses purpose.

tempestīva is vocative singular, agreeing with the implied addressee Chloe to whom the imperative *dēsine* is directed.

FYI

Line 3 *montibus āviīs* is the first of three ablative phrases in the poem in which the preposition *in* is to be inferred. "Understood" prepositions like this are common in Latin poetry.

Line 5 *Caveat lector!!* The 3ʳᵈ declension ending set on the *vēr-* base indicates that *vēris* is a form of *vēr, vēris,* n. ("spring") and not *vērus, -a, -um* ("true, real, genuine").

Line 9 An infinitive to express purpose rather than an *ut/nē* subjunctive clause is not uncommon in poetry.

Horace *Odes* I.23.1–12 Modified

This is another poem about love, one in which the poet considers the girl's feelings as well as his own. Horace tries to persuade a young girl, likened to a fearful and skittish fawn, that her fears are groundless. The first stanza introduces the simile, the second expands it with more detail, and the last rejects the comparison.

> **Vītās mē inuleō similis, Chloē,**
> **quaerentī pavidam mātrem**
> **montibus āviīs nōn sine vānō**
> **metū aurārum et silvae.**
>
> 5   **Nam seu adventus vēris**
> **foliīs mobilibus inhorruit,**
> **seu viridēs lacertae rubum dīmōvērunt,**
> **et corde et genibus tremit.**
>
>   **Atquī nōn ego tē frangere persequor,**
> 10 **ut tigris aspera Gaetūlusve leō:**
> **tandem dēsine, tempestīva virō,**
> **mātrem sequī.**

ANALYSIS AND COMPREHENSION OF THE LATIN TEXT

1. Who is/are fearing what in lines 1–4?

2. Another poetic device is the practice of asserting something by denying its opposite, or understatement, often increased with a negative word. We may, for example, describe something as "not bad" rather than claim it is "good." This device is called LITOTES. Find an example in line 3.

3. What are the indications of spring's arrival in lines 5–8? What words in these lines reinforce the idea of movement?

LITERARY ANALYSIS AND DISCUSSION

1. To what human fears may the animals' fears in lines 1–4 correspond?

2. The subject of *tremit* (line 8) is unspecified. How does this fact affect the meaning of the second stanza?

3. Does the poet's word choice *frangere* in line 9 correspond well with the meaning of the name Chloe? Why or why not?

Roman girl

RAPID REVIEW #7: ENCLITICS

See Bennett, 6.1, 84.2, 86.3 and 142.4 or Gildersleeve, 15, 102, 454, and 476 for a more detailed discussion of this topic.

The term "enclitic" derives from Greek words meaning to "lean upon." Consequently, an enclitic is a little appendage or particle leaning upon the end of a word. Two enclitics are seen commonly, the others infrequently.

COMMONLY SEEN:

1. *-que* meaning "and." The enclitic indicates a close connection between two items often viewed as one entity in two parts: cf. the English expressions "love and marriage," "pb and j," "Ben and Jerry's," etc.

2. *-ne* added to a sentence's initial emphatic word indicates that the sentence is a question simply seeking information. Neither a "Yes" nor a "No" answer is implied or expected: cf. the English questions "Did you see him?" or "Are you going, too?"

INFREQUENTLY SEEN:

3. *-ve* meaning "or." This is a different way of expressing the same "or" as *vel*.

4. *-met* or 5. *-pte* on a personal pronoun or possessive adjective add emphasis or intensity: cf. *egomet:* "I myself" or *suōpte gladiō:* "by his very own sword."

PRACTICE

Each of these exercises contains an enclitic. <u>Underline</u> the enclitic in each exercise, and then <u>translate</u> 1–4.

1. Tēne provincia narrat esse bellam?
2. . . . tigris aspera Gaetūlusve leō . . .
3. Quālēs lacertōs vīdī tetigīque!
4. Amāns in montēs flūminaque alta ībit.

The following six examples come from the first book of Vergil's epic poem, *The Aeneid*.

5. Arma virumque canō.
6. Tantaene animīs caelestibus īrae sunt?
7. Pallasne exūrere classem Argīvum potuit?
8. Urbs fuit dīves opum studiīsque asperrima bellī.
9. Tantane fīdūcia generis vestrī vōs tenuit?
10. Durāte, et vōsmet rēbus secundīs servāte!

Horace *Odes* III.9.1–16 Modified

READING VOCABULARY

Line 1   **donec** – *conj.:* so long as, while

      gratus – **gratus, -a, -um:** pleasing, welcome; grateful (+ dative)

   2   **quisquam** – **quisquam, quidquam,** *indefinite adj.:* any, some

      potior – **potior, -ius:** more able, more powerful, preferable, better

   3   **bracchia** – **bracchium, - ī,** *n.:* arm, forearm (elbow to wrist)

      cervīcī – **cervix, cervīcis,** *f.:* neck, nape of the neck

   4   **beatior** – **beātus, -a, um:** happy, i.e. blessed; prosperous; fertile; wealthy, rich; sumptuous

      viguī – **vigeō, vigēre, viguī, _____:** flourish, thrive, be vigorous

   5   **arsistī** – **ardeō, ardēre, arsī, arsūrus:** burn, be on fire (with passion)

   6   **Īlia** – Ilia, also known as Rhea Silvia, was the legendary mother of Romulus and Remus.

   9   **Thressa** – **Thressus, -a, -um:** Thracian, from Thrace

   10   **docta** – **doctus, -a, -um:** learned, skilled, taught

      modōs – **modus, -ī,** *m.:* (musical) measure, rhythm; the pl. can mean "poetry."

      citharae – **cithara, -ae,** *f.:* lyre

11   **pro** – *prep.* + *abl.:* for, on behalf of, in place of

      metuam – **metuō, metuere, metuī, metūtum:** fear, dread, be afraid of

12   **animae** – **anima, -ae,** *f.:* breath, spirit, soul, life; darling

      superstitī – **superstes (superstitis),** *adj.:* standing over, surviving, outliving; perhaps here "and let her survive"

      parcent – **parcō, parcere, pepercī, parsūrus:** spare, forebear, refrain from injuring (+ dative)

      Calais – name of Lȳdia's new boyfriend, who was the son of a man named Ornytus who lived in Thūriī, a town in southern Italy. The reference balances the earlier mention of Thrace: perhaps his mention of an exotic place-name (Thrace) elicits a comparable one from her.

14   **face** – **fax, facis,** *f.:* torch, fire-brand, taper

      mūtuā – **mūtuus, -a, -um:** shared, mutual, reciprocal

      torret – **torreō, torrēre, torruī, tostum:** burn, parch (with heat)

15   **bis** – *adv.:* twice

      patiar – **patior, patī, passus sum:** experience, undergo, suffer, endure; allow, permit

READING HELPS

Line 1   *quisquam,* though normally an indefinite pronoun, here is used as an adjective equivalent to *ullus, -a, -um.*

   4   The *-ior* ending on *beātior* indicates the comparative degree of this adjective. An ablative of comparison such as *rēge* here is commonly found with this degree. There are several pairs like this in VIII-A and VIII-B.

   5   *aliā* should be taken as an ablative of cause, not an ablative of comparison.

   7   *multī nōminis* is a "genitive of description." cf. SELECTION II, Reading Help 1–4.

   10   The *dulcēs modōs* are in the accusative case because they state in what *respect* Chloe is skilled or learned (*docta*).

11 ff.   Pay close attention to the conjugation and tense of the verb forms *metuam, parcent,* and *patiar.*

FYI

Line 10   Such an "accusative of respect" is a common poetic construction, especially pertaining to parts of the body, while the "ablative of respect" (or "specification") is typical in prose.

Line 11   *Caveat lector!!* Carefully distinguish the forms of *morior, morī, mortuus sum* ("die") from *moror, morārī, morātus sum* ("delay"), from *mors, mortis,* f. ("death"), from *mora, -ae,* f. ("delay") and from *mōs, mōris,* m. ("custom, habit").

Horace *Odes* III.9.1–16 Modified

This light-hearted poem presents the reader with an imaginary, good-natured dialogue between former lovers, an unnamed man (Horace himself?) and a woman (a courtesan?) named Lȳdia whose name suggests an eastern origin. In the poem, the man speaks first and the two lovers then alternate stanzas as they explore the idea of a possible reconciliation. Each speaks the same number of lines and tries to "cap" or "one-up" what the other has just said. Imaginary poetic dialogues are common in ancient pastoral poetry (e.g. Vergil's *Eclogues*), but not in lyric. In fact, this is Horace's only poem in this form. The poem's twenty-four lines have been divided into two assignments or sections: lines 1–16 in SELECTION VIII-A and lines 17–24 in SELECTION VIII-B.

"Donec tibi grātus eram
nec quisquam iuvenis potior
bracchia candidae cervīcī dabat,
beātior Persārum rēge viguī."

5   "Donec aliā nōn magis arsistī
neque Lȳdia post Chloēn erat,
Lȳdia multī nōminis,
clārior Rōmānā Īliā viguī."

"Thressa Chloē mē nunc regit,
10   docta dulcēs modōs et citharae sciēns,
prō quā morī nōn metuam,
sī fāta animae superstitī parcent."

"Calais, fīlius Thūrīnī Ornytī,
face mūtuā mē torret,
15   prō quō bis morī patiar,
sī fāta puerō superstitī parcent."

"citharae sciens . . ."

RAPID REVIEW #8: COMPARISON OF ADJECTIVES

See Bennett, 71–75 or Gildersleeve, 86–90 for a more detailed discussion of this topic.

An adjective is said to have three degrees: Positive (e.g. "wide"), Comparative (e.g. "wider") and Superlative (e.g. "widest").

1. The **positive** degree normally is the vocabulary/dictionary entry: *altus, -a, -um*: "high, tall"; *fortis, -e*: "strong, brave," etc.

2. The **comparative** degree of an adjective is regularly formed by adding *-ior* (m. and f.), *-ius* (n.) to the base of the positive degree. The base of the positive degree is obtained by dropping the nominative, singular, feminine ending. Thus, for *altus, alta, altum* the comparative degree is *altior, altius* and for *fortis, forte* the comparative degree is *fortior, fortius*.

   a. A comparative degree adjective is declined with the ending set of a regular 3rd declension noun, e.g. *rēx, lēx* or *corpus*. Note that the entire *-ior* form serves as the base for all genders.

altior	altius	altiōrēs	altiōra
altiōris	altiōris	altiōrum	altiōrum
altiōrī	altiōrī	altiōribus	altiōribus
altiōrem	altius	altiōrēs	altiōra
altiōre	altiōre	altiōribus	altiōribus

   b. The comparative degree has many possible meanings: "_____r, more _____, rather _____, too _____, quite _____, somewhat _____."

   c. Remember that a comparative degree word is often followed by a *quam* ("than") and a word in the same case as the compared noun. When the two nouns compared are in the nominative or accusative, an "ablative of comparison" may be substituted for the *quam* + the second noun in the same case. *Meus frāter est fortior quam tuus*. or *Meus frāter est fortior tuō*. cf. Rapid Review # 5.

   d. Some irregularly formed comparatives must be memorized.

3. The **superlative** degree is usually formed by adding *-issimus, -a, -um* to the base of the positive degree. Thus, for *altus, alta, altum* the superlative degree is *altissimus, -a, -um* and for *fortis, forte* it is *fortissimus, -a, -um*.

   a. The superlative degree has several possible meanings: "_____st, most _____, very _____, exceedingly _____," etc.

   b. *-er* adjectives (e.g. *pulcher, pulchra, pulchrum; celer, celeris, celere*, etc.) form their superlative degree by adding *-rimus, -a, -um* to the nominative, singular, masculine form: e.g. *pulcherrimus, -a, -um* or *celerrimus, -a, -um*.

   c. Six *-lis, -le* adjectives (*facilis, -e; difficilis, -e; similis, -e; dissimilis, -e; gracilis, -e; humilis, -e*) form their superlative degree by adding *-limus, -a, -um* to the positive's base: e.g. *facillimus, -a, -um* or *humillimus, -a, -um*. Other adjectives looking the same (e.g. *utilis, -e*) form their superlative degree as usual: *utilissimus, -a, -um*.

   d. Some irregularly formed superlatives must be memorized.

4. Some irregularly compared adjectives must be memorized, especially:

bonus, -a, -um	melior, -ius	optimus, -a, -um
malus, -a, -um	peior, -ius	pessimus, -a, -um
magnus, -a, -um	maior, -ius	maximus, -a, -um
parvus, -a, -um	minor, minus	minimus, -a, -um
multī, -ae, -a	plūrēs, plūra	plūrimī, -ae, -a

PRACTICE

1. Declension Drill: Singular and Plural

ager latior	domus latior	flūmen latius

2. Comparison Drill: give the other two degrees for these adjectives.

asper, -era, -erum	_____	_____
_____	beātior, -ius	_____
_____	_____	optimus, -a, -um
brevis, -e	_____	_____
_____	facilior, -ius	_____
_____	_____	grātissimus, -a, -um
miser, -era, -erum	_____	_____
_____	mōbilior, -ius	_____
_____	_____	nigerrimus, -a, -um
parvus, -a, -um	_____	_____
_____	pulchrior, -ius	_____
_____	_____	simillimus, -a, -um

Horace *Odes* III.9.17–24 Modified

READING VOCABULARY

Line 17 **prisca – priscus, -a, -um:** old, former, ancient

18 **dīductōs – dīdūcō, dīdūcere, dīduxī, dīductum:** separate, draw apart

iugō – iugum, -ī, *n.:* yoke, bond

aēneō – aēneus, -a, -um: bronze

cōgit – cōgō, cōgere, coēgī, coactum: force, compel; drive/gather together, collect, assemble

19 **flāva – flāvus, -a, -um:** reddish-blonde, flame-colored, fiery

excutitur – excutiō, excutere, excussī, excussum: shake out, extinguish, cast out, jilt

20 **reiectae – reiciō, reicere, reiēcī, reiectum:** throw back, drive back, reject

patet – pateō, patēre, patuī, _____: be open, lie open, be agape

21 **quamquam –** *a concessive conj.:* although

sīdere – sīdus, sīderis, *n.:* a star, constellation

22 **levior – levis, -e:** light, slight, quick (to change); here perhaps "fickle"

cortice – cortex, corticis, *m.:* a cork, piece of bark (or rind)

īrācundior – īrācundus, -a, -um: easily upset, irascible, prone to anger, hot-tempered, passionate

23 **improbō – improbus, -a, -um:** uneven, rough, stormy, troublesome

Hadria – Hadria, -ae, *m.:* the notoriously stormy Adriatic Sea, located between Italy and Greece

24 **libēns – libēns (libentis):** willing, ready, glad

obeam – obeō, obīre, obiī, obitum: die; **mortem obīre:** go to (meet) death, die

READING HELPS

Line 17 *Venus* illustrates the poetic device of METONYMY.

18 *dīdūctōs* is used substantively, with an *eōs* (the boy and Lȳdia) understood.

23–24 *amem* and *obeam* are "potential" subjunctives: "I would . . ."

FYI

Line 17 Be careful to distinguish the forms of *red + eō >redeō, redīre, rediī, reditum* ("go back, return") from *red + dō >reddō, reddere, reddidī, redditum* ("give back, return"). ALL forms *of reddō* have the distinguishing characteristic -dd-; NONE of the forms *of redeō* have this consonant cluster.

20–22 *Caveat lector!!* Be careful to distinguish the forms of *pateō, patēre, patuī, _____* ("be open, lie open, be agape") from *patior, patī, passus sum* ("permit, allow; suffer, undergo"), and the forms of *levis, -e* ("light, slight, quick") from those of *lēvis, -e* ("smooth, slippery; delicate, tender").

"Lydiae ianua patet . . ."

Horace *Odes* III.9.17–24 Modified

"Quid sī prisca Venus redit
dīductōsque iugō aēneō cōgit?
Sī flāva Chloē excutitur
20   reiectaeque Lȳdiae iānua patet?"

"Quamquam sīdere pulchrior ille est,
tū levior cortice et īrācundior
improbō Hadriā, tēcum vīvere amem,
tēcum libēns obeam."

ANALYSIS AND COMPREHENSION OF THE LATIN TEXT

1. How many personal names are there in the poem? Whose is significantly absent?

2. Who is meant by the phrase *prisca Venus* in line 17?

3. Is *reiectae Lȳdiae* in line 20 genitive or dative? What difference does it make for the poem's meaning?

4. A common poetic device is ELLIPSIS, the omission of a word or phrase easily inferred from the context or association with a nearby line. In the last stanza, what word must the reader supply for *tū . . . Hadriā*? (Hint: it's a verb!)

LITERARY ANALYSIS AND DISCUSSION

1. What may be the implication of the absence mentioned in #1 above?

2. Line 4's reference *Persārum rēge* was a proverbial one for riches, power, success, etc. and line 8's *Rōmānā Īlia* for fame and renown. Look carefully at the word choice and emphasis of each speaker throughout the poem's exchanges, and note what love involved for each one: for him, it was power and control, but for her, popularity and ardency. Are these characterizations universal, i.e. still in evidence, or are they author, time and culture specific?

3. What is the significance of the fact that the poet chose *aliā* rather than *alterā* in line 5?

4. A *fax*, such as that mentioned in line 14, was often used in a Roman wedding ritual. Consequently, what overtone is added to Lȳdia's reply?

RAPID REVIEW #9: CONDITIONAL SENTENCES

See Bennett, 301–306 or Gildersleeve, 589–602 for a more detailed discussion of this topic.

Definition: A conditional sentence is a compound sentence that consists of a <u>condition</u> (the "if" clause, called the *protasis*) and a <u>conclusion</u> (the "then" clause, called the *apodosis*). Conditional sentences are categorized into three types, depending on the degree of reality of the condition.

1. The first category are conditions of **fact** (also called "real" or "simple" conditions) in which nothing is implied about the reality of the condition. Being factual or real, they are in the **indicative** mood, **any tense**, and are translated normally.

    Example: *Sī adest, nōn abest.*   If he is present, he is not absent.

2. The second category are **imaginary** conditions (also called "future less vivid" or "should/would" conditions). Being imaginary, they are in the **subjunctive** mood, **present tense**, and are translated with a "should" and a "would."

    Example: *Sī adsit, nōn absit.*   If he <u>should</u> be present, he <u>would</u> not be absent.

3. The third category are conditions **contrary to fact.** Being unreal, they are in the **subjunctive** mood.

    a. When such a condition is in the <u>present time</u>, the verbs are in the **imperfect** subjunctive and are translated with a "were" and "would."

      Example: *Sī adesset, nōn abesset.*   If he <u>were</u> present (but he's not), he <u>would</u> not be absent.

    b. When such a condition is in the <u>past time</u>, the verbs are in the **pluperfect** subjunctive and are translated with a "had" and a "would have."

      Example: *Sī adfuisset, nōn afuisset.*   If he <u>had</u> been present (but he wasn't), he <u>would</u> not <u>have</u> been absent.

PRACTICE

a. Analyse the verbs in each of these sentences to determine the type of condition:
   1. simple/factual
   2. imaginary/future less vivid/should-would
   3. unreal/contrary to fact-pres./contrary to fact-past
b. Then translate the sentence.
   1. Sī fāta animae eius parcunt, Lȳdia morī nōn metuit.
   2. Sī fāta animae eius parcent, Lȳdia morī nōn metuet.
   3. Sī fāta animae eius parcant, Lȳdia morī nōn metuat.
   4. Sī fāta animae eius parcerent, Lȳdia morī nōn metueret.
   5. Sī fāta animae eius pepercissent, Lȳdia morī nōn metuisset.
   6. Nisi prisca Venus redit, flāva Chloē nōn excutitur.
   7. Nisi prisca Venus redībit, flāva Chloē nōn excutiētur.
   8. Nisi prisca Venus redeat, flāva Chloē nōn excutiātur.
   9. Nisi prisca Venus redīret, flāva Chloē nōn excuterētur.
   10. Nisi prisca Venus redīsset, flāva Chloē nōn excussa esset.

These sentences are more generic, but offer additional practice opportunities.

11. Si bonōs mōrēs habēs, tē laudāmus.

12. Si bonōs mōrēs habēbis, tē laudābimus.

13. Si bonōs mōrēs habeās, tē laudēmus.

14. Si bonōs mōrēs habērēs, tē laudārēmus.

15. Si bonōs mōrēs habuissēs, tē laudāvissēmus.

16. Nisi vēritātem petimus, sapientiam nōn invenīmus.

17. Nisi vēritātem petēmus, sapientiam nōn veniēmus.

18. Nisi vēritātem petāmus, sapientiam nōn veniāmus.

19. Nisi vēritātem peterēmus, sapientiam nōn invenīrēmus.

Horace *Odes* III.26.1–12 Modified

READING VOCABULARY

Line 1 **vīxī – vīvō, vīvere, vīxī, vīctum:** live, be alive

nūper – *adv.:* recently, lately, not long ago

idōneus – idōneus, -a, -um: fit, suitable, able-bodied, appropriate (+ dative)

2 **mīlitāvī – mīlitō, mīlitāre, mīlitāvī, mīlitātum:** serve as a soldier

3 **pariēs – pariēs, parietis, m.:** a (house) wall

4 **dēfunctum – dēfungor, dēfungī, dēfunctus sum:** be discharged, retired, done with, finished

barbiton – a *Greek accusative singular form:* a lyre, a lute

5 **laevum – laevus, -a, -um:** left (here, left of the image of the deity)

latus – latus, lateris, n.: side, flank

custōdit – custōdiō, custōdīre, custōdīvī (or -iī), custōdītum: watch, guard, protect

7 **lūcida – lūcidus, -a, -um:** bright, full of light, glowing, burning

funālia – funāle, -is, n.: torch

vectēs – vectis, -is, m.: a lever, crowbar, prybar

arcūs – arcus, -ūs, m.: bow

8 **oppositīs – oppōnō, oppōnere, opposuī, oppositum:** hinder, oppose, block

foribus – foris, -is, m.: a door, gate, entrance; *pl.,* a set of double-doors, i.e. two side-by-side panels which made up the *ianua.*

minācēs – minax (minācis), *adjective:* threatening, menacing (+ dative)

9 **Cyprum –** Cyprus was an island central to worship of Venus, who reportedly was born in the sea nearby.

10 **Memphin –** another Greek accusative form: Memphis was a city in Egypt, site of temple to Venus

Sīthonia – the Sīthoniī were a tribe in Thrace, an area thought by ancients to be cold, snowy, uncivilized, and barbaric.

nive – nix, nivis, *f.:* snow

carentem – careō, carēre, caruī, _____: lack, be without (+ abl.)

11 **sublīmī – sublīmis, -e:** raised, uplifted

flagellō – flagellum, -ī, n.: lash, whip

12 **arrogantem – arrogāns (arrogantis):** scornful, arrogant, proud, overbearing

READING HELPS

Line 3 The soldier-lover's *arma* are detailed in line 7.

5 The antecedent of *quī* is *pariēs.*

marīnae is an appropriate description for Venus not only because of the standard story of her birth from the sea's foamy froth, told already by the archaic Greek poet Hesiod, but also because Horace often associates the ideas of storms and disasters with the sea (and the parallel to the "stormy voyage through the sea of Love" is apparent).

6 The imperative *pōnite* is addressed to some imagined servants who are accompanying the lover-soldier-poet.

7 *funālia* are torches not of pine branches (= *facēs* and for indoor use) but of rope soaked in wax, animal fat or tar, which apparently gave a brighter and longer-lasting light and were used outside when a stronger and more intense light was required.

Line 7 emphasizes that the lover-soldier must be prepared to press his "attack" against opposition with all the weapons at his disposal: fire, steel, and bow.

9–12 Note in the final stanza that the deity is identified not by name but by referring to her various spheres of power or shrines. Of course, in this poem she is specifically named earlier in line 5.

12 A causal idea perhaps is present in *arrogantem* (which really is a present active participle).

FYI

Line 6 *Caveat lector!!!* Macrons make a difference! The adverb *hīc* ("here") can be distinguished from the demonstrative adjective/pronoun *hic, haec, hoc* ("this") by the macron above the "i."

Horace *Odes* III.26.1–12 Modified

In this semi-serious poem, Horace adopts the pose of an experienced lover confronted with the reality that he should, like a soldier past his prime, retire from competition in love's battles. The reader needs to imagine that the poet with a small entourage of slaves has gone to Chloe's door to serenade her but has not been welcomed and admitted as usual. He deduces that he has lost it, and that his career as a lady's man is finished; consequently, he pretends to dedicate his well-used "gear," now retired, to his patron deity.

> Vīxī nūper idōneus puellīs
> et mīlitāvī nōn sine glōriā.
> Nunc hic pariēs arma habēbit
> dēfunctumque bellō barbiton,
>
> 5 quī laevum marīnae Veneris latus
> custōdit. Hīc, hīc pōnite
> lūcida fūnālia et vectēs et arcūs
> oppositīs foribus minācēs.
>
> Ō dīva, quae beātum Cyprum tenēs
> 10 et Memphin Sīthoniā nive carentem,
> Ō rēgīna, sublīmī flagellō tange
> Chloēn semel arrogantem.

ANALYSIS AND COMPREHENSION OF THE LATIN TEXT

1. What poetic device is found in the phrase *nōn sine glōriā?* in *hīc, hīc?* in *bellō barbiton?*

2. Line 5 is an example of the common word order arrangement called CHIASMUS, in which words are arranged in an ABBA or "bookend" order. Here it is accusative: genitive::genitive:accusative. What words also form a CHIASMUS in lines 7–8? in line 10?

3. If the lover is a soldier, what type is he? an infantryman? a cavalryman? an artilleryman? Check out his weapons for a clue.

LITERARY ANALYSIS AND DISCUSSION

1. Chloe seems to have been giving the poet the "brush off." Consider what is known about Chloe from earlier reading and decide if any details in this poem are explained or better understood by what was read about her then.

2. Is the poem's bold metaphor of love as war effective? Be sure to support your response with specific textual references.

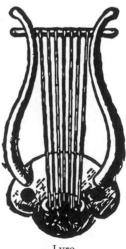

Lyre
"defunctum . . . barbiton"

3. Consider the last stanza's *tange:*

   a. What is the effect of the poet's use of an imperative rather than a more polite subjunctive form like *tangās?*

   b. What does the poet seek by this imperative? Is it punishment for the girl? If so, how may she have offended Venus? Is it to make her fall in love with him again so as to effect her return to him?

4. The adverb *semel* can be read either with the earlier *tange* or with the *arrogantem* right next to it. Think about the ambiguous implications of the different readings, and decide which reading makes more sense.

5. Was the poet serious when he offered a farewell to the battles of love?

RAPID REVIEW #10: DEPONENT VERBS

See Bennett, 112–114 or Gildersleeve, 113, 128, 163–167, 220 for a more detailed discussion of this topic.

1. These verbs have laid aside (*dē- pōnō*) most of their active forms. They are passive in form BUT active in their meanings. Hence, a useful mnemonic for deponent verbs is **PFAM: P**assive **F**orm, **A**ctive **M**eaning.

2. Deponent verbs are recognizable in a vocabulary, for they have but three principal parts, the passive equivalents of the usual first three.

   Examples: **arbitror, arbitrārī, arbitrātus sum:** think

   polliceor, pollicērī, pollicitus sum: promise

   loquor, loquī, locūtus sum: say, speak

   gradior, gradī, gressus sum: move, go

   orior, orīrī, ortus sum: arise, rise

3. Three areas deserve close attention:

   a. Deponent verbs have four <u>participles</u>, a mix of active and passive forms AND meanings:

FORM		MEANING
PRESENT ACTIVE	loquēns (loquentis)	saying (active meaning)
PERFECT PASSIVE	locūtus, -a, -um	having said **(n.b. pass. form, act. meaning)**
FUTURE ACTIVE	locūtūrus, -a, -um	about to say (active meaning)
FUTURE PASSIVE	loquendus, -a, -um	about to be said (passive meaning)

   b. They have three <u>infinitives</u>, a similar mix:

FORM		MEANING
PRESENT PASSIVE	loquī	to say **(n.b. pass. form, act. meaning)**
PERFECT PASSIVE	locūtus, -a, -um esse	to have said **(n.b. pass. form, act. meaning)**
FUTURE ACTIVE	locūtūrus, -a, -um esse	to be about to say (active meaning)

c. It is still easy to recognize an imperfect subjunctive verb in Latin; to form one, however, one needs to take the given present infinitive (e.g., **loquī**), convert it to what its active form would be if it were to exist (e.g. **loquere**), and then attach the usual passive personal endings. The chart below illustrates the deponent subjunctive forms.

		PRESENT	IMPERFECT	PERFECT	PLUPERFECT
Sing.	1	loquar	**loquere*r***	locūtus, -a, -um sim	locūtus, -a, -um essem
	2	loquāris	**loquerē*ris***	locūtus, -a,-um sīs	locūtus, -a, -um essēs
	3	loquātur	**loquerē*tur***	locūtus, -a, -um sit	locūtus, -a, -um esset
Plur.	1	loquāmur	**loquerē*mur***	locūtī, -ae, -a sīmus	locūtī, -ae, -a essēmus
	2	loquāmini	**loquerē*mini***	locūtī, -ae, -a sītis	locūtī, -ae, -a essētis
	3	loquantur	**loquere*ntur***	locūtī, -ae, -a sint	locūtī, -ae, -a essent

PRACTICE

A. **Write synopses as directed for the following deponent verbs.**

1. 1st pl. of **hortor, hortārī, hortātus sum:** urge

2. 3rd sing. of **patior, patī, passus sum:** endure

3. 3rd pl. of **experior, experīrī, expertus sum:** try, attempt

B. **Form and translate the 4 participles and 3 infinitives of** *sequor, sequī, secūtus sum:* **follow.**

C. **Translate these contextual sentences containing deponent verb forms.**

1. Haec ego sīc singula confiteor.

2. Hic pariēs arma habēbit dēfunctumque barbiton.

3. Nōn ego tē frangere persequor.

4. Tandem dēsine matrem sequī.

5. Nox abiit nec tamen diēs orta est.

MAJOR REVIEW #2

FORMATION, DECLENSION, TRANSLATION AND BASIC USAGES OF PARTICIPLES

See Bennett, 336–337 or Gildersleeve, 282–283, 409–410, 251–252, 664–667 for a more detailed discussion of this topic.

A. **Definition.** A participle is a verbal adjective, a verb form that modifies (describes) a noun or pronoun: the <u>running</u> girl, the <u>lost</u> coin, a book <u>worth reading (fit-to-be-read)</u>. As an adjective, it agrees in **case, number and gender;** as a verb form, it has **tense** and **voice.**

B. **Forms.**

PARTICIPLE	TIME EXPRESSED	FORMATION	DECLENSION	TRANSLATION	IDENTIFYING LETTERS
PRESENT ACTIVE	same time as main verb	present stem + *-ns* (*-nt-* in gen. and other cases)	like 3rd declension adjectives	_____ ing	**-NT-** (PRESE**NT**)
		docēns, docentis, capiēns, capientis		teaching, taking	
PERFECT PASSIVE	time prior to main verb	4th princ. part stem + *-us, -a, -um*	like 1st and 2nd decl. adjectives	having been _____ed, _____ed	
		doctus, -a, -um, captus, -a, -um		(having been) taught, (having been) seized	
FUTURE ACTIVE	time after main verb	4th princ. part stem + *-ūrus, -a, -um*	like 1st and 2nd decl. adjectives	about to _____	**-ŪR-** (FUTURE)
		doctūrus, -a, -um, captūrus, -a, um		about to teach, about to take	
FUTURE PASSIVE/ GERUNDIVE	time after main verb	present stem + *-ndus, -a, -um*	like 1st and 2nd decl. adjectives	about to be _____ed	**-ND-** (GERU**ND**IVE)
		docendus, -a, -um, capiendus, -a, -um		about to be taught, about to be taken	

FORM DRILL

1. Give in the nominative singular and literally translate the participles of these verbs, taken from SELECTIONS VII–IX.

   a. dō   b. torreō   c. regō   d. excutiō   e. patior

2. Identify the form (tense and voice) and literally translate these participles.

a. vītāns	f. vītātus	k. vītātūrus	p. vītandus
b. doctus	g. doctūrus	l. docendus	q. docēns
c. fractūrus	h. frangendus	m. frangēns	r. fractus
d. sequendus	i. sequēns	n. secūtus	s. secūtūrus
e. custōdiēns	j. custōdītus	o. custōdītūrus	t. custōdiendus

C. **Usages**

   Usage 1. As a regular adjectival modifier—even as a substantive; any of the four participles.

   a. *Puellam currentem spectābāmus.* We were watching the running girl.

   b. *Librum āmissum invēnit.* He found the [having been] lost book.

   c. *Puerum cursūrum vīdī.* I saw the about-to-run boy (as he was about to run).

   d. *Librum legendum invēnit.* He found a fit-to-be-read book (which was worth reading).

   Translating Modifying Participles: Expansions

   As is clear from the last two examples, sometimes a literal translation leads to awkward English. Consequently, one often must EXPAND the participle (or participial phrase) into an English clause. When this is done, be VERY CAREFUL to show the correct time relationship between the participle and its main verb. Listed below are the various types of expansion clauses most frequently used; which one to use in a given sentence depends upon the sentence's context and the individual reader. Though the example has a perfect passive participle in it, the same principles apply to all four participles.

   Librum āmissum invēnit.

LITERAL	He found the	[having been] lost book.
RELATIVE	He found the book	which had been lost.
TEMPORAL		after (when) it had been lost.
CAUSAL		because (since) it had been lost.
CONCESSIVE		although it had been lost.
		(This one usually is signaled by a *tamen* in the main clause.)
CONDITIONAL		if it had been lost.
COORDINATE		The book had been lost and he found it.

   Note that not all these possiblilities work equally well for this sentence and, in fact, the literal version works well here. Note too that each expansion has retained the correct time relationship: the participle's action is shown as having occurred prior to that of the main verb.

FYI

Since a participle is a verb form, it often is found at the end of its phrase. This means that any words between the participle and the earlier word it modifies are likely to depend on the participle and be part of its phrase. Before you undertake the following drill, take the time to note the phrasing.

REGULAR ADJECTIVAL MODIFIER DRILL

Translate each contextual sentence twice: first with its participle literally rendered, then with its participle expanded into an appropriate clause.

1. Quis fuit vir adversus Lesbiam sedēns?
2. Lesbiam dulce ridentem audīre poteram.
3. Puella, nec bellō pede nec nigrīs oculīs habēns, cum Lesbiā nostrā comparārī nōn dēbet.
4. Catullus, Quintiam esse formōsam negāns, Lesbiam laudābat.
5. Nōs ipsī, rūmōrēs senum unīus assis aestimantēs, vīvāmus atque amēmus!
6. Mulier, sē nullī quam amantī nūbere malle dīcēns, nōn semper est crēdibilis.
7. Scēlesta puella, nihil rogāta, dolēbit.
8. Puella ab Catullō iam obdūrante nōn rogābitur—et dolēbit.
9. Chloē, mātrem quaerēns, poētam vītāvit.
10. Ab inuleō, vānum metum aurārum habente, māter quaesīta est.

Usage 2. As part of an ablative absolute; any of the four participles.

a. Definition: Despite a rather imposing name, the ablative absolute construction is not that unfamiliar in actual practice. English, for example, has a similar construction, seen in a sentence such as "He being the teacher, the students knew that they would learn a lot." Note that the opening phrase, "He. . ." is nominative case ("He" not "Him"); that is because English expresses such phrases, syntactically unrelated to (or absolute from) the main clause, as "nominative absolutes." Ancient Greek does the same thing in the genitive case, and Latin does it in the ablative. So a noun or pronoun that has no grammatical function in or relationship to the main clause (not the subject, object, etc.) is said to be ABSOLUTE from the main clause and is in the ablative case in Latin. Any modifier of that noun or pronoun must be in agreement, i.e. also ablative. Such an absolute phrase, a noun or pronoun and its modifier, will be in the ablative case in Latin and comprises an "ablative absolute." Consider the following Latin example:

Pecūniā inventā, puer ad urbem revēnit.
The money having been found, the boy returned to the city.

Note that the noun (*pecūniā*) modified by the participle (*inventā*) has no role or function in the main clause (*puer ad urbem revēnit*). Consequently, the noun is absolute (separate) grammatically from the main clause. Therefore it is in the ablative case, and the participle modifying it naturally agrees in case, number and gender.

b.   Types of ablative absolutes

(1) Noun/Pronoun + Participle. This is by far the most common.

   Usually it is a perfect passive participle:

   Pecūniā inventā, puer ad urbem revēnit.

   The money having been found, the boy returned to the city.

   Sometimes it is a present active participle:

   Eō regnum petente, timeō.

   This man seeking royal power, I am afraid.

   Infrequently it is a future active or passive participle:

   Duce regnum petītūrō, populus fuit īrātus.

   A general about to seek royal power, the populace was irate.

   Regnō ab duce petendō, populus fuit īrātus.

   Royal power about to be sought by the general, the populace was irate.

(2) Noun/Pronoun + Noun/Pronoun (with implied participle of "being").

   Caesare duce, hostēs superābimus.

   Caesar (being) the general, we shall overcome the foe.

   Eīs nostrīs sociīs, nullōs hostēs timēmus.

   These (being) our allies, we fear no foe.

(3) Noun/Pronoun + Adjective (with implied participle of "being").

   Caesare īrātō, mīlitēs trepidābant.

   Caesar (being) angry, the soldiers used to tremble.

Translating Ablative Absolutes: Expansions

Like other participial expressions, an ablative absolute may need to be expanded to attain idiomatic English. Any of those mentioned earlier may be used EXCEPT THE RELATIVE. Be sure to maintain the correct time relationship.

ABLATIVE ABSOLUTE DRILL

Translate each contextual sentence twice: first with its participle literally rendered, then with its participle expanded into an appropriate clause.

1.   Tē aspectā, Lesbia, mea lingua torpet.
2.   Lesbiā tēcum comparātā, saeculum est vērē insapiēns et infacētum!
3.   Quintiā esse formōsā negātā, Lesbia ab omnibus laudāta est.
4.   Omnibus rūmōribus senum unīus assis aestimātīs, vīvāmus atque amēmus!
5.   Multīs mīlibus basiōrum factīs, nē quis malus nōbīs invidēre possit.
6.   Virō cupiente, mulier nōn crēdenda est.
7.   Catullō obdūrātō, puella dolēbit.
8.   Inuleus, rubīs ā lacertīs dīmōtīs, et corde et genibus tremit.
9.   Nullō iuvene tibi potiōre, beātior Persārum rēge viguī.
10. Filiō Ornȳtī mē torrente, bis morī patiar.

Usage 3. As part of a periphrastic construction. Future participles only.

   a.   Definition: Though saddled with an even more intimidating title, this construction is merely a "roundabout way of speaking:" cf. *peri,* "around"; *phrasis,* "speaking."

   b.   Types of periphrastics

      (1) The First or Active Periphrastic: a Future ACTIVE Participle + a form of *sum.*

Aquam portātūrus est.	He is going (about) to carry the water.
Aquam portātūra fuit.	She was going (about) to carry the water.

         Note that these are simply the "roundabout" way of saying

Aquam portābit.	(S)he will carry the water.

      (2) The Second or Passive Periphrastic: a Future PASSIVE Participle + a form of *sum.* This is a common way of expressing the idea of OBLIGATION or NECESSITY. The agent by whom the action has to be done is expressed in the DATIVE case (Dative of Agent) in most instances.

Aqua puellae portanda est.	The water IS to be carried by the girl. i.e. The water HAS TO BE (MUST BE) carried by the girl.

PERIPHRASTIC DRILL

Translate these contextual sentences.

1.   Quintia cum Lesbiā nostrā nōn comparanda est.

2.   Lesbia omnibus laudanda fuit.

3.   Sī fāta puerō parsūra sunt, bis morī passūra sum.

4.   Omnēs rūmōrēs senum unīus assis aestimandī sunt.

5.   Omnia, quae mulier cupidō amantī dīcit, in ventō et rapidā aquā tibi, Catulle, scribenda sunt.

6.   Scēlestae puellae labella nullī basianda sunt.

7.   Mater tibi, virō tempestīvae, Chloē, nōn sequenda est.

8.   Hic pariēs arma mea habitūrus est.

9.   Ianuā Lȳdiae patente, flāva Chloē excutienda est.

10.   Chloē, Ō rēgīna, sublīmī flagellō tangenda est.

REVIEW DRILL: ALL PARTICIPLE USAGES

Reread the following sentences (or parts of sentences); then identify each participle's form, modification and usage.

SELECTION I.	1–5	Ille mī pār esse deō vidētur, ille, sī fās est, mī superāre dīvōs vidētur, quī sedēns adversus identidem tē spectat et tē dulce ridentem audit, quod omnēs sensūs mihi miserō ēripit:
SELECTION V.	3–4	Dīcit: sed quod mulier cupidō amantī dīcit in ventō et rapidā aquā scrībere oportet.
SELECTION VI.	8	At tū, Catulle, destinātus obdūrā.
SELECTION VII.	1–4	Vītās mē inuleō similis, Chloē, quaerentī pavidam mātrem montibus āviīs nōn sine vānō metū aurārum et silvae.
SELECTION VIII-A.	9–12	"Thressa Chloē mē nunc regit, docta dulcēs modōs et citharae sciēns, prō quā morī nōn metuam, sī fāta animae superstitī parcent."
SELECTION VIII-B.	17–18, 21–24	"Quid sī prisca Venus redit dīductōsque iugō aēneō cōgit? "Quamquam sīdere pulchrior ille est, tū levior cortice et īrācundior improbō Hadriā, tēcum vīvere amem, tēcum libēns obeam."
SELECTION IX.	3–4, 6b–8, 9–12	Nunc hic pariēs arma habēbit dēfunctumque bellō barbiton, Hīc, hīc pōnite lūcida fūnālia et vectēs et arcūs oppositīs foribus minācēs. Ō dīva, quae beātum Cyprum tenēs et Memphin Sīthoniā nive carentem, Ō rēgīna, sublīmī flagellō tange Chloēn semel arrogantem.

Publius Ovidius Naso provides several details of his life in two autobiographical poems, written when he was in exile, that have come down to us. He reports that he was born into a prosperous equestrian family on March 20, 43 BCE, in Sulmo, about ninety miles east of Rome. He says that he had a brother who was exactly one year older.

Rome was still in a political and societal uproar (cf. Introductions to Catullus and Horace). Julius Caesar had been assassinated just one year previously, and political leadership remained unsettled. During the year of Ovid's birth, Octavian, Antony and Lepidus formed the Second Triumvirate, and the proscription and death of Cicero occurred.

After the break-up of the Second Triumvirate, civil war broke out between the supporters and armies of Octavian and those of Antony. The climactic battle of Actium in 31 BCE established Octavian's supremacy when Ovid was only twelve and still attending school in his hometown. As Ovid entered his teens and was sent to Rome for further study, Octavian was solidifying his power and control. The poet writes that his father wanted and expected a public career for him, so he studied the liberal arts and especially oratory with two of the city's finest teachers. By his own account, he undertook additional study in Athens, like Catullus and Horace, and then traveled through Asia Minor and Sicily before returning to Rome. He reports that his passion for poetry finally caused him to reject the political career desired by his father and to turn toward Rome's young social and literary elites. Their interest, now that Octavian was in firm political control, had turned from politics to amusement. The emperor's daughter Julia was their leader.

In his late teens, Ovid developed close friendships with Tibullus and Propertius, two prominent and promising young poets. Soon these three, along with the poetess Sulpicia, were taken into a literary circle whose patron was Valerius Messala Corvinus, a prominent and distinguished leader in government. Corvinus seems to have encouraged the literary pursuits of Ovid and his circle of friends the way that Maecenas had encouraged Horace's circle, and Cato, Catullus' circle. Ovid's first two marriages were brief and unsuccessful; his third lasted life-long. He had one daughter.

M. Antony

The emperor and the poet seem often to have been at odds. Octavian, on the one hand, aimed to restore Rome's traditional values in order to reinvigorate a community devastated by social and political turmoil for over a century. Ovid, on the other hand, was gaining public recognition and acclaim for his poetry that often seemed to undermine this aim. He first published the *Amōrēs*, a collection of love poems, and then the *Herōidēs*, a series of letters from deserted mythological heroines to the lovers who had deserted them. In 2 BCE his *Ars Amātōria* arrived, a mock instructional manual on the art of loving. "Professor" Ovid offered practical advice to both sexes on how to woo and win a lover. In his *Dē Medicāmine Faciēī* he dealt with how properly to use make-up. With their playful attitude toward love, marriage and traditional values, these poems may have been viewed by Octavian as satiric criticism of his endeavor. In short, the emperor was probably not amused.

Furthermore, the appearance and popularity of Ovid's amatory poetry coincided with a personal and political scandal that touched the imperial household. Octavian had just discovered that his daughter Julia was embroiled in an affair with a son of Mark Antony, and he was outraged. He may have felt betrayed **personally** when Julia appeared to "thumb her nose" at him by taking up with the son of his political enemy. He may have felt betrayed **politically** when she appeared to flaunt his government's efforts to restore public morality. At any rate, he disinherited and banished her.

In a possible attempt to regain the emperor's good will, Ovid soon undertook the *Remedia Amōris*, poems on how to resist love. He then started his *Fastī*, a series of poems that celebrate the origins of important days in the Roman calendar. At the same time, he was starting the *Metamorphōsēs*, mythological stories united by the theme of change. Then, in 8 BCE, disaster struck. While Ovid was on the island of Elba, word came that he had been banished by Augustus to exile at Tomis, far from Rome on the coast of the Black Sea.

Precise, precipitating reasons for the banishment are unclear. Ovid himself, in one of his poems, mentions a *carmen et error*: many scholars read ongoing imperial displeasure over the *Ars Amātōria* in the *carmen*. Some think that the *error* involved the scandal of Julia's disgrace. Others suspect that the poet favored Germanicus as Augustus' successor over Tiberius, who was favored by Octavian's wife Livia, and was the ultimate appointee.

In any case, Ovid spent the rest of his days at Tomis, miserable at being away from friends and family, and desperately longing for the attractions of Rome. Yet, he was poetically productive. His *Tristia* are, as the name suggests, sad poems about the grimness of life in Tomis, and the *Epistulae ex Pontō* are verse-letters of lament to his friends and relatives back home. When Augustus died in 14 CE and was succeeded by Tiberius, from whom there was no hope of pardon, Ovid knew that Rome was forever lost. He died three years later in 17 CE.

Tiberius

SELECTIONS X–XI are taken from one of those early works, the *Amōrēs*. Written during his youth, they tend to reflect a light-hearted and playful attitude toward love and life. Ovid assumes the *persōna* of a lover: witty, urbane, emotionally detached from the situation. He was perhaps more interested in displaying his poetic skill and versatility with clever artistry than in describing the details of heartfelt love with sensitivity and accuracy. His elegiac couplets tend to be self-contained, with a complete thought occurring within the two lines. There is frequent ENJAMBMENT as the first line of the couplet spills over into the second. Consequently, it is very helpful to note the complete thought groups of words by paying close attention to where the full-stop punctuation (period, colon or semicolon) is located. Ovid switches from past to present tenses as he tries to enhance the vividness of his presentation. He often pairs an adjective in the middle of the line with a noun at the line's end.

Some students find it helpful to compare Catullus and the emotional intensity of his expression with the composer Rachmaninov, Horace and his careful control of each word's placement with the composer Beethoven, and Ovid with his glitter, glitz and brilliance with the composer Mozart.

TIMELINE FOR OVID

43 BCE	O. born; 2nd Triumvirate; death of Cicero
31 BCE	Actium
24/23 BCE	O. rejects politics; publication of *Amōrēs*
20s BCE	O. in Rome, Athens, Sicily, and Rome
8 CE	O. banished to Tomis
14 CE	death of Augustus
17 CE	O.'s death

Ovid

Ovid *Amōrēs* I.5.1–12 Modified

READING VOCABULARY

Line 1 **aestus – aestus, -ūs,** *m.:* heat, sultriness

exēgerat – ex + agō>exigō, exigere, exēgī, exactum: drive out

2 **levanda – levō, levāre, levāvī, levātum:** lift, raise, lighten, relieve, ease

3 **adaperta** (*a variant of* **aperta**) **– aperiō, aperīre, aperuī, apertum:** open, spread apart

4 **quāle – quālis, -e:** of what sort? of what kind?

ferē – *adv.:* generally, usually, as a rule

5 **crepuscula – crepusculum, -ī,** *n.:* twilight, dimness, obscurity; *pl.* may mean darkness

sublūcent – sublūceō, sublūcēre: shine faintly, shimmer, glimmer

6 **orta – orior, orīrī, ortus sum:** rise, arise

7 **verēcundīs – verēcundus, -a, -um:** shy, bashful, modest, reserved

praebenda – praebeō, praebēre, praebuī, praebitum: offer, provide, supply, present

8 **pudor – pudor, pudōris,** *m.:* (sexual) shame, modesty, decency, propriety

latebrās – latebrae, -ārum, *f.:* hiding places

vēlāta – vēlō, vēlāre, vēlāvī, vēlātum: veil, cover, dress, clothe

10 **dīvidua – dīviduus, -a, -um:** separated, divided, perhaps "parted" here

comā – coma, -ae, *f.:* hair

tegente – tegō, tegere, texī, tectum: cover, protect, shelter, hide

11 **quāliter –** *adv.:* in like fashion, just like

fāmōsa – fāmōsus, -a, -um: much talked of, famous, renowned; infamous; slanderous, libelous

thalamus – thalamus, -ī, *m.:* bedroom

īsse – eō, īre, iī, itum: go

READING HELPS

Line 1 The idea in the first half of the line is that "There was heat." We would say "It was hot out." The idea in the second half is that the day had "driven out" or "passed" mid-day.

2 *levanda:* the future passive participle "to be relieved/eased," "which needed to be relieved/eased."

3 The second half of this line clearly illustrates a double ELLIPSIS.

Think back to what was learned about the shape of a Roman door (*forēs*) in SELECTION IX, line 8. A Roman *fenestra* had a similar set of parallel shuttered panels.

4–6 Each of these lines contains a description of the quality of light that Ovid envisions: *quāle . . . solent, quālia . . . fugiente,* and *aut ubi . . . orta.*

Note that the ablative absolute at the end of the line, *Phoebō fugiente,* contains a present active participle instead of the more common perfect passive participle.

7 Though one might logically tend to take *puellīs* as a dative of agent due to the proximity of the passive periphrastic *est praebenda,* it really is a dative of reference and retains its "to (for)" meaning.

8 It is uncommon to find a present, rather than a future, infinitive depending on a form of *spērō.*

Gildersleeve's *Latin Grammar* (531.n.4) states that the present occurs "when an immediate realization of the hope is anticipated."

10 "Proper" women in Rome wore their hair up, so the poet is giving some information about Corinna here.

dīviduā comā . . . tegente: another ablative absolute containing a present active participle. Note the macrons, for they clarify which words are part of the ablative absolute with *tegente* and which words are the direct object of this participle.

11 *īsse, iisse,* and *īvisse* all are found as the perfect active infinitive form for *eō.*

11–12 Semiramis (also spelled Semeramis and Sameramis) and Lāis were legendary for their beauty. The Greek courtesan Lāis lived during the time of the Peloponnesian War in the late fifth century BCE; Semiramis may allude to a famous Assyrian queen from the third millennium BCE.

12 This line contains an example of SYNCHESIS, a pattern in which words are arranged in an ABAB or "interlocked" order: *Lāis:multīs::amāta:virīs.* This arrangement often stresses the close relationship of the pairs making up the phrase. Cf. CHIASMUS in SELECTION IX's Reading Help 10.

Ovid *Amōrēs* I.5.1–12 Modified

In this rather specific poem, Ovid describes a summer afternoon's enjoyable siesta. He sets the scene, describes Corinna's coming—and what follows. The poem's twenty-six lines have been divided into two assignments or sections: lines 1–12 in SELECTION X-A and lines 13–26 in SELECTION X-B.

> Aestus erat, et diēs mediam hōram exēgerat;
>   adposuī mediō membra levanda torō.
> Pars fenestrae adaperta fuit, pars altera clausa,
>   quāle lūmen silvae habēre ferē solent,
> 5 quālia crepuscula sublūcent Phoebō fugiente
>   aut ubi nox abiit nec tamen diēs orta.
> Illa lux verēcundīs puellīs est praebenda,
>   quā timidus pudor latebrās habēre spēret.
> Ecce! Corinna venit, tunicā vēlāta recinctā,
> 10 dīviduā comā candida colla tegente,
> quāliter in thalamōs fāmōsa Semiramis īsse
>   dīcitur et Lāis multīs amāta virīs.

"Ecce! Corinna venit . . ."

RAPID REVIEW #11: IRREGULAR VERBS *EŌ, FERŌ, FĪŌ, SUM* AND *VOLŌ* (and their compounds)

See Bennett, 124, 126, 129–130, 132 or Gildersleeve, 116–119, 168–169, 171, 174 for a more detailed discussion of this topic.

The irregularities for these verbs occur primarily in their principal parts and present systems (those tenses built upon the present infinitive stem—present, imperfect and future indicative, and present and imperfect subjunctive). Their passive voice (if any) and perfect systems are regular in their formation. Most of the irregularities are found in the present indicative and subjunctive; as a result, these must be carefully studied.

PRINCIPAL PARTS

eō, īre, īvī (or iī), itum: go

fīō, fierī, (factus sum): become, be made, happen

volō, velle, voluī, _____: be willing, want
    (+ complem. infin.)

nō(n vo)lō >nōlō, nolle, nōluī, _____: be unwilling

ferō, ferre, tulī, lātum: carry, bear, endure

sum, esse, fuī, futūrus: be

ma(gis vo)lō >mālō, malle, māluī, _____:
    be more willing, want more, prefer

Present Indicatives

ĪRE	FERRE	ESSE	VELLE	NOLLE	MALLE	FIERĪ
eō	ferō	sum	volō	nōlō	mālō	fīō
īs	fers	es	vīs	nōn vīs	māvīs	fīs
it	fert	est	vult	nōn vult	māvult	fit
īmus	ferimus	sumus	volumus	nōlumus	mālumus	fīmus
ītis	fertis	estis	vultis	nōn vultis	māvultis	fītis
eunt	ferunt	sunt	volunt	nōlunt	mālunt	fiunt

Present Subjunctives

ĪRE	FERRE	ESSE	VELLE	NOLLE	MALLE	FIERĪ
eam	feram	sim	velim	nōlim	mālim	fīam
eās	ferās	sīs	velīs	nōlīs	mālīs	fīās
eat	ferat	sit	velit	nōlit	mālit	fīat
eāmus	ferāmus	sīmus	velīmus	nōlīmus	mālīmus	fīāmus
eātis	ferātis	sītis	velītis	nōlītis	mālītis	fīātis
eant	ferant	sint	velint	nōlint	malint	fīant

SYNOPSES DRILL

Here is an example in the 3rd person, singular, indicative and subjunctive of *sum*. Study it; then compose similar synopses as suggested below.

est, erat, erit, fuit, fuerat, fuerit; sit, esset, fuerit, fuisset

1. *eō* – 1st, plural, active
2. *volō* – 2nd, plural, active
3. *ferō* – 3rd, plural, active and passive
4. *nōlō* – 1st, singular, active
5. *mālō* – 2nd, singular, active
6. *fīō* – 3rd, singular, active

Translate these contextual sentences that contain irregular verb forms.

1. Mea mulier nullī quam mihi nūbere mavult.
2. Sōlēs occidere et redīre possunt.
3. Quis tē nunc adībit?
4. Rediitne prisca Venus?
5. In thalamōs formōsa Semiramis īsse dīcitur.

Ovid *Amōrēs* I.5.13–26 Modified

READING VOCABULARY

Line 13 **dēripuī – dē + rapiō>dēripiō, dēripere, dēripuī, dēreptum:** snatch, tear, rip off or down (from her shoulders)

rāra – rārus, -a, -um: thin, scanty i.e. filmy, gauzy

nocēbat – noceō, nocēre, nocuī, nocitum: harm, injure (+ dative)

15 **tamquam –** *conj.:* as, just as, just like

16 **aegrē –** *adv.:* with difficulty, barely

prōditiōne – prōditiō, -iōnis, *f.:* betrayal, treason

17 **vēlāmine – vēlāmen, -minis,** *n.:* clothing, garment, veil

nusquam – *adv.:* nowhere

menda – menda, -ae, *f.:* flaw, blemish, fault

23 **singula – singulī, -ae, -a:** single, one at a time, individual

referō – referō, referre, rettulī, relātum: bring back, renew, repeat, announce, report, relate, tell

25 **cētera – cēterus, -a, -um:** the other, remaining, rest (of)

lassī – lassus, -a, -um: weary, tired, worn-out, spent

requiēvimus – requiescō, requiescere, requiēvī, requiētum: begin to rest up, recover

ambō – ambō, ambae, ambō: both, the two

READING HELPS

Line 13 The significance of the prepositional prefix of *dēripuī* becomes apparent in lines 18–22.

The idea of *multum . . . nocēbat* is close to "nor was it doing much harm;" i.e. it wasn't concealing much because of its fish-net composition.

14 The idea of *tegī pugnābat* approximates "she was struggling to be covered." Note that the infinitive is used here to express purpose. cf. SELECTION VII, Reading Help 4.

15 The opening *quae* is a "connecting" relative and equivalent to *et ea*.

The rather awkward *ita . . . tamquam quae . . .* may be rendered "in such a way (or as if) she . . ." or "like a woman who . . ."

17 Be sure to note the mood of *stetit*. The indicative indicates that *ut* means "as, when" rather than "that, in order that" as with the subjunctive.

pōnō in poetry often has the idea of *dēpōnō*, to put down, lay aside.

19–22 The omitted lines enumerate in quite specific detail Corinna's physical attractions.

25 A *-scō* suffix on a verb like *requiescō* adds the idea of inception: "I begin to rest."

26 Note the independent "jussive" subjunctive construction of *prōveniant*: "let them/may they come forth, turn out or happen."

FYI

Line 2 **SYNECDOCHE** is a poetic device by which a part stands for, or represents, a whole, so decide what this line *mediō . . . torō* tells the reader about the poem's dramatic situation. When the arrangement of words also pictures the meaning of these words, the poetic technique is called **FRAMING**. Here is a well-known example from Vergil's *Aeneid*:

Hīc vastō rex Aeolus antrō sedet. "Here king Aeolus sits in a vast cave," where king Aeolus is visually seen within the *vastō . . . antrō*.

Ovid *Amōrēs* I.5.13–26 Modified

Dēripuī tunicam; nec multum rāra nocēbat
    sed illa tamen tunicā tegī pugnābat;
15 quae cum ita pugnāret tamquam quae vincere nollet,
    victa est nōn aegrē prōditiōne suā.
    Ut stetit ante oculōs nostrōs positō vēlāmine,
    nusquam in tōtō corpore menda fuit:
    . . . .
20 . . . .
    . . . .
    . . . .
    Singula quid referam? Nil nōn laudābile vīdī,
    et nūdam pressī usque ad corpus meum.
25 Cētera quis nescit? Lassī requiēvimus ambō.
    Mediī diēs sīc mihi saepe prōveniant!

ANALYSIS AND COMPREHENSION OF THE LATIN TEXT

1. Concerning line 3's ELLIPSIS, what words are to be inferred from the first half of the line?

2. List the eight participles in the poem and identify the usage of each. Note that *adaperta* and *clausa* with *est* constitute normal passive voice compound verb forms.

3. Note line 2's CHIASTIC word arrangement: ABBA. In this example, note the word picture portrayed: i.e. what are in the middle of the narrow Roman bed?

4. In lines 1–12, which words form an ALLITERATION? a METONYMY? a CHIASMUS? a SYNCHESIS?

5. Consider line 9: what sort of *tunica* would Corinna likely be wearing for this visit?

6. What is the significance of the plural forms *thalamōs* and *multīs . . . virīs* in lines 11–12?

7. In lines 13–26, which words form an HYPERBOLE? a LITOTES?

8. Is the *cum* clause in line 15 expressing circumstance, cause or concession?

9. What type of questions are *Singula quid referam?* and *Cētera quis nescit?* cf. SELECTION VI, Analysis and Comprehension of the Latin Text, 4.

LITERARY ANALYSIS AND DISCUSSION

1. Line 10 discusses Corinna's hairstyle. What are its implications? What nationality do you think she is? From what social background?

2. Some readers interpret line 14's phrase *tegī pugnābat* as Corinna putting on a "show of modesty." Is there evidence in the poem to support this view?

3. In view of all the 1st person, singular verb forms in the poem, what may be the significance of the <u>plural</u> possessive adjective *nostrōs* (rather than *meōs*)?

RAPID REVIEW #12: FORMATION AND COMPARISON OF ADVERBS

See Bennett, 75–77, 140, 157 or Gildersleeve, 91–93, 439–449 for a more detailed discussion of this topic.

Positive, comparative, and superlative degree adverbs usually are formed from their corresponding degree adjectives, as illustrated in the chart below.

	POSITIVE FORM	POSITIVE MEANING	COMPARATIVE FORM	COMPARATIVE MEANING	SUPERLATIVE FORM	SUPERLATIVE MEANING
1st and 2nd Declension Adjectives	Adj. stem + -*ē*	____ ly	Adj. stem + -*ius* Same as neuter comparative adjective	rather, quite, too, or more ____ ly	Adj. stem + -*issimē* *r*-stems: add -*rrimē* *l*-stems: add -*llimē*	most ____ly or very ____ly
3rd Declension Adjectives	Adj. Stem + -*iter*					
Examples: pulcher, pulchr/a, pulchrum	pulchrē	beautifully	pulchrius	more beautifully	pulcherrimē	most beautifully
fort/is, forte	fortiter	bravely	fortius	more bravely	fortissimē	most bravely
gracil/is, gracile	graciliter	gracefully	gracilius	more gracefully	gracillimē	most gracefully

Some irregularly formed and/or compared adverbs must be memorized, especially:

bonus, -a, -um:	bene	melius	optimē
malus, -a, -um:	male	peius	pessimē
magnus, -a, -um:	magnopere	magis	maximē
parvus, -a, -um:	parum, paulum	minus	minimē
multus, -a, -um:	multum	plūs	plūrimum

PRACTICE

Comparison Drill: give the three degrees for the adverbs derived from these adjectives.

asper, -era, -erum   _____   _____   _____

beātus, -a, -um   _____   _____   _____

bonus, -a, -um   _____   _____   _____

brevis, -e   _____   _____   _____

facilis, -e   _____   _____   _____

gratus, -a, -um   _____   _____   _____

miser, -era, -um   _____   _____   _____

mōbilis, -e   _____   _____   _____ niger, -gra, -grum   _____   _____   _____

parvus, -a, -um   _____   _____   _____

pulcher, -chra, -chrum   _____   _____   _____

similis, -e   _____   _____   _____

Translate these contextual sentences.

1. Ōtium et regēs et beātās urbēs prius perdidit.

2. Simul atque Catullus Lesbiam aspexit, lingua eius celeriter torpuit et tenuis flamma sub artūs tardē dēmānāvit.

3. Salvē, amīca Formiānī, nec ōre siccō puella nec sanē nimis ēlegante linguā.

4. Da mī bāsia mille – quam celerrimē!

5. Quam saepe fulsēre vērē candidī tibi solēs!

6. Dōnec nōn aliā magis arsistī, Rōmānā viguī clarior Īliā.

7. Quam fēminam poēta plurimum amābat?

8. Prōveniant mediī sīc mihi saepius diēs!

9. Chloē et corde et genibus maximē tremēbat.

10. Catullus cōgitāvit poēma ab amīcō venustissimē incohātum esse.

Ovid *Amōrēs* I.9.1–14 Modified

READING VOCABULARY

Line 1 **mīlitat – mīlitō, mīlitāre, mīlitāvī, mīlitātum:** *intr.* to be a soldier, to do military service

castra – castra, -trōrum, *n. pl.:* a camp (military)

3 **aetās – aetās, -tātis,** *f.:* age, time of life

bellum – bellum, -ī, *n.:* war

habilis – habilis, -e: handy, suitable, fit

convenit – conveniō, convenīre, convēnī, conventum: be suitable, fit, be appropriate, suit

4 **turpe – turpis, -e:** ugly, loathsome, repulsive, shameful, disgusting

senex – senex (senis): aged, old

senīlis – senīlis, -e: of old people, of an old man; aged; senile

5 **animōs – animus, -ī,** *m.:* mind, soul, spirit; *pl.* may = morale, courage

ducēs – dux, ducis, *m.:* leader, guide; general

6 **sociō – socius, -ī,** *m.:* partner, companion, ally

7 **pervigilant – pervigilō, pervigilāre, pervigilāvī, pervigilātum:** keep watch, be on guard all night

uterque – uterque, utraque, utrumque: each (of two)

9 **officium – officium, -ī,** *n.:* duty, task, office

10 **strenuus – strenuus, -a, -um:** restless, keen, vigorous

fine – finis, -is, *m.:* end, limit; boundary, border

exemptō – eximō, eximere, exēmī, exemptum: take away, remove

11 **adversos – adversus, -a, -um:** opposing, obstructing, standing in the way

duplicāta – duplicō, duplicāre, duplicāvī, duplicātum: double

nimbō – nimbus, -ī, *m.:* cloudburst, rainstorm

12 **flūmina – flūmen, -minis,** *n.:* river, stream

congestās – congerō, congerere, congessī, congestum: heap up, pile up

exteret – exterō, exterere, extrīvī, extrītum: rub out, wear away, trample

13 **frēta – frētum, -ī,** *n.:* strait, sea

tumidōs – tumidus, -a, -um: swollen, swelling, causing swells (waves)

causābitur – causor, causārī, causātus sum: give or plead (the accus.) as an excuse or reason

14 **sīdera – sīdus, sīderis,** *n.:* star, constellation

apta – aptus, -a, -um: fit, suitable (+ dat.)

verrendīs – verrō, verrere, verrī, versum: pass over, skim, sweep, scour, row (over the waters)

READING HELPS

Line 2 The addressee Atticus is not identifiable with any certainty.

4 *turpe* is used substantively, "a disgraceful thing."

5 *petiēre* is a common poetic contraction of *petīvērunt*; the subject is *ducēs*.

6 *sociō*: in apposition to *virō*. In English, we might say "in a male partner/companion."

7 *requiescit*, as in the previous poem, contains an inceptive idea.

8 Unlike line 4's single ELLIPSIS, this line has a double ELLIPSIS: two words are to be inferred from the immediate context.

9 *mitte* is used here in the sense of "send away, send ahead or dispatch."

10 The singular form *fine* is uncommon.

12–14 *ille* is the subject of the three verbs in these lines, and is modified by *pressūrus*.

14 *sīdera* is used as a METONYMY for "weather."

verrendīs is a future passive participle (also known as a gerundive) modifying *aquīs*. Treat as an English gerund: "for skimming the waves."

FYI

Lines 3–6 *Caveat lector!!* Be careful to distinguish: *aetās* ("age") from *aestās* ("summer") from *aestus* (a "boiling motion" of flame, hence "heat, sultriness" or of water, hence "wave, surge, flood;" the adverb *quoque* ("also, too, as well") from the pronoun form *quōque* (from *quisque*: "each" (of three or more); the adjective *bellus, -a, -um* ("pretty, lovely, charming") from the noun *bellum,-ī,* n. ("war"); and the related pair of adjectives *senex* ("old, aged") and *senīlis, -e* ("characteristic of an old person").

Line 7 While *ambō* means "both," *uterque, utraque, utrumque* means "each (of two)" and *quisque, quidque* "each (of three or more)."

Line 8 *Caveat lector!!* Be careful to distinguish the 3rd declension noun *foris, -is,* f. ("doorway") from the 2nd declension's *forum, -ī,* n. ("forum, marketplace").

Ovid *Amōrēs* I.9.1–14 Modified

As in Horace *Odes* III.26, Ovid in this poem explores the idea of love as war. Atticus, the addressee, apparently has contended that a lover and a soldier are not at all similar; the one is dedicated to leisure while the other fights for his life. Here, Ovid strives to convince Atticus that the lover and the soldier face similar challenges. Both must be young, fit, endure long tours of duty, and overcome various physical hardships. The poem's thirty-two lines are broken up into two assignments or sections: lines 1–14 in SELECTION XI-A and lines 15–32 in SELECTION XI-B.

> Mīlitat omnis amāns, et Cupīdō sua castra habet;
> > Attice, crēde mihi, mīlitat omnis amāns.
> Aetās, quae bellō est habilis, Venerī quoque convenit.
> > Turpe senex mīles, turpe senīlis amor.
> 5 Quōs animōs ducēs petiēre in mīlite fortī,
> > hōs bella puella petit in sociō virō:
> pervigilant ambō, terrā requiescit uterque;
> > ille forēs dominae servat, at ille ducis.
> Mīlitis officium longa est via: mitte puellam,
> 10 strenuus amāns fīne exemptō sequētur;
> ībit in adversōs montēs duplicātaque nimbō
> > flūmina, ille congestās exteret nivēs,
> nec freta pressūrus tumidōs causābitur Eurōs
> > aut sīdera quaeret apta verrendīs aquīs.

Roman legionary

RAPID REVIEW #13: DEMONSTRATIVE ADJECTIVES *HIC, ISTE, ILLE, IS* AND *ĪDEM*

See Bennett, 87, 246–248 or Gildersleeve, 103–104, 305–308 for a more detailed discussion of this topic.

These "pointing" words, particularly *hic, ille* and *is*, are found everywhere as one reads Latin. Their forms, especially in the singular, must be thoroughly familiar. Like any adjective, they may be used substantively and then function as pronouns.

	ADJECTIVAL USAGE	MEANING	SUBSTANTIVE/ PRONOUN USAGE	MEANING
hic	hic vir	this man	hic	this (m) one, he
iste	ista fēmina	that woman	ista	that (f) one, she
ille	illud oppidum	that town	illud	that (n) one, it
is	eī mīlitēs	these/those soldiers	eī	they (m)
īdem	eaedem mulierēs	the same women	eaedem	the same, they (f)

The important and very real differences among these demonstratives lie in their connotations:

hic, haec, hoc   an emphatic or forceful "this"; it is associated with the speaker and hence has the idea of "this near me/us" or "this of mine/ours."

iste, ista, istud   an emphatic or forceful "that"; it is associated with the person(s) addressed and hence has the idea of "that near you" or "that of yours." It often has a pejorative or negative overtone as well. It is declined exactly like **ille, illa, illud** (see chart below).

ille, illa, illud   an emphatic or forceful "that"; it is associated with the person(s) talked about and hence has the idea of "that near him/her/it/them" or "that of his/hers/its/theirs."

is, ea, id   an unemphatic or weak "this, that"; it is associated with a person or thing already mentioned earlier or about to be mentioned later. Some compare it to the English definite article "the." It serves as the usual substitute for the missing 3rd person personal pronoun.

īdem, eadem, idem   an emphatic or forceful "the same." This word is a composite of the forms of *is, ea, id* and the suffix -*dem*. Note that the -*dem* suffix is NOT declined.

The forms of *ille* and *iste* are identical, and *īdem, eadem, idem* is a compound of *is, ea, id*. Practically speaking, therefore, one should know the forms of *hic, ille* and *is* to negotiate successfully the Latin demonstratives. Note how regular the plurals are.

hic	haec	hoc	ille	illa	illud	is	ea	id
hūius	hūius	hūius	illīus	illīus	illīus	eius	eius	eius
huic	huic	huic	illī	illī	illī	eī	eī	eī
hunc	hanc	hoc	illum	illam	illud	eum	eam	id
hōc	hāc	hōc	illō	illā	illō	eō	eā	eō
hī	hae	haec	illī	illae	illa	eī	eae	ea
hōrum	hārum	hōrum	illōrum	illārum	illōrum	eōrum	eārum	eōrum
hīs	hīs	hīs	illīs	illīs	illīs	eīs	eīs	eīs
hōs	hās	haec	illōs	illās	illa	eōs	eās	ea
hīs	hīs	hīs	illīs	illīs	illīs	eīs	eīs	eīs

PRACTICE

Form Drill. Decline the following combinations in the singular and plural.

1. hic puer   haec puella   hoc oppidum
2. ille rex   illa lex   illud mare
3. is exercitus   ea rēs   id cornū

Translate these contextual sentences containing demonstratives.

1. Ille mī pār esse deō vidētur, . . .
2. Haec ego sīc singula confiteor.
3. Quamquam sīdere pulchrior ille est, tū levior cortice, . . .
4. Nunc hic pariēs arma habēbit . . .
5. Illa lux verēcundīs puellīs est praebenda.
6. Sed illa tamen tunicā tegī pugnābat.
7. Hōs animōs bella puella petit in sociō virō.
8. Ille forēs dominae servat, at ille ducis.
9. Ille amāns congestās nivēs exteret.
10. Ille gravēs urbēs, hic dūrae līmen amīcae obsidet.

Ovid *Amōrēs* I.9.15–32 Modified

READING VOCABULARY

Line 15 **frīgora – frīgus, -goris,** *n.:* cold, chill, frost

16 **nivēs – nix, nivis,** *f.:* snow

densō – densus, -a, -um: thick, heavy

imbre – imber, imbris, *m.:* rainstorm, rain; sometimes hail, snow

mixtās – misceō, miscēre, miscuī, mixtum: mix, mingle

perferet – perferō, perferre, pertulī, perlātum: bear through, suffer, undergo, endure

17 **speculātor – speculātor, -tōris,** *m.:* spy, scout

infestōs – infestus, -a, -um: hostile, deadly

18 **hoste – hostis, -is,** *m.:* a foe, an enemy

dūrae – dūrus, -a, -um: hard, harsh, cruel

līmen – līmen, līminis, *n.:* threshold, lintel; doorway, entrance; outset, beginning

20 **obsidet – obsideō, obsidēre, obsēdī, obsessum:** lay siege to, besiege

21 **sopōrātōs – sopōrātus, -a, -um:** sound asleep, buried in sleep, unconscious

profuit – prosum, prodesse, profuī, profutūrus: be advantageous, helpful, useful

22 **caedere – caedō, caedere, cecīdī, caesum:** cut, cut down, strike, slay

inerme – inermis, -e: unarmed, defenseless

23 **agmina – agmen, -minis,** *n.:* a marching column (of an army), army

Rhēsī: Rhesus, a Thracian leader, brought his forces to fight on behalf of the Trojans against the Greeks.

24 **dēseruistis – dēserō, dēserere, dēseruī, dēsertum:** leave, forsake, abandon, desert

25 **nempe –** *adv.:* to be sure, certainly, surely, without any doubt

marītōrum – marītus, -ī, *m.:* husband, spouse

ūtuntur – ūtor, ūtī, ūsus sum: use, employ (+ abl., here *somnīs*).

26 **sopītīs – sopiō, sopīre, sopīvī, sopītum:** put to sleep, stun, knock unconscious

27 **vigilum – vigil, vigilis,** *m.:* a watchman, sentinel, guard. cf. *pervigilant* in line 7.

catervās – caterva, -ae, *f.:* a squad, troop

30 **iacēre – iaceō, iacēre, iacuī, _____:** lie, lie low, be flat, extend, spread out

31 **quīcumque – quīcumque, quaecumque, quodcumque:** whoever, whatever-presumably the Atticus of line 2.

dēsidiam – dēsidia, -ae, *f.:* laziness, idleness, inactivity

32 **ingeniī – ingenium, -ī,** *n.:* intellect, character, spirit, nature

experientis – experiēns (experientis): active, enterprising

READING HELPS

Line 18 The root idea of *rīvālis* comes from *rīvus*: a river, channel or stream. One who also used the same channel or stream was a neighbor, a possible meaning for *rīvālis*. The idea was transferred to one who used the same mistress' "channel," and hence acquired the overtone of a "rival."

20 Note who is who: the *hic* is the *mīles*; the *ille* is the *amāns*.

22 Though *manus* generally means "hand," sometimes it means a "handful" or little "band."

24 *captī equī* are vocative plural, as the poet in his imagination addresses the horses (*dēseruistis*).

25 *ūtuntur* is from *ūtor*, "I use" (+ abl.)

26 *sopītīs . . . hostibus* is probably best taken as an ablative absolute.

transīre: the infinitive phrase in this line is the subject of the impersonal expression *opus (est)* in line 28, which also takes the genitives *mīlitis et . . . amantis:* "there is need of, it is necessary for (the genitive of the person) to (do the infinitive)."

30 *quōsque* is not a form of *quisque* but correlative to *victīque:* _____*que . . .* _____*que.*

negēs: a "relative clause of characteristic" subjunctive construction: "(those whom) you would deny . . ."

32 *dēsinat:* a "jussive" subjunctive construction: "should cease, let him cease . . . "

ingeniī . . . experientis is a genitive of quality/description. cf. SELECTION II, Reading Help 1–4.

Ovid *Amōrēs* I.9.15–32 Modified

15 Quis nisi vel mīles vel amāns et frīgora noctis
    et nivēs densō imbre mixtās perferet?
Mittitur speculātor alter infestōs in hostēs,
    in rīvāle, ut hoste, alter tenet oculōs.
Ille gravēs urbēs, hic dūrae līmen amīcae
20   obsidet; hic portās frangit, at ille forēs.
Saepe sopōrātōs invādere profuit hostēs
    et caedere armātā vulgus inerme manū.
Sīc fera Thrēiciī cecidērunt agmina Rhēsī,
    et dominum dēseruistis, captī equī.
25 Nempe marītōrum somnīs ūtuntur amantēs
    et sua sopītīs hostibus arma movent.
Custōdum transīre manūs vigilumque catervās
    mīlitis et miserī semper amantis opus.
Mars dubius, nec certa Venus: victīque resurgunt
30   quōsque negēs umquam posse iacēre, cadunt.
Ergō dēsidiam quīcumque vocābat amōrem,
    dēsinat: ingeniī est experientis Amor.

FYI

Line18   *Caveat lector!!* Distinguish *hostis* ("stranger; enemy, foe") from *hospes* ("host, guest"). The English derivatives "hostility" and "hospitality" will assist.

Line 19   *Caveat lector!!* Distinguish *līmen* ("threshold") from *lumen* ("light"). The English derivatives "sub-liminal" and "illuminate" will assist.

Lines 22–30   *Caveat lector!!* Carefully distinguish forms of:

cadō, cadere, cecidī, cāsum ("fall, sink") from *caedō, caedere, cecīdī, caesum* ("cut, slay"). The English derivatives "occasion" and "incision, herbicide" will assist; and *iaceō, iacēre, iacuī, _____* ("lie flat, be open") from *iaciō, iacere, iēcī, iactum* ("throw, toss"). The English derivatives "adjacent" and "projectile" will assist.

Line 25   There are five deponent "PUFFV" verbs that take the ablative:

potior, potīrī, potītus sum: get, get possession of, seize, win, gain

ūtor, ūtī, ūsus sum: make use of, use, employ

fruor, fruī, frūctus sum: enjoy

fungor, fungī, fūnctus sum: perform, fulfil, discharge, pay

vescor, vescī, _____: feed upon, feast upon, eat

ANALYSIS AND COMPREHENSION OF THE LATIN TEXT

1. Though line 1's reflexive possessive adjective agrees with *castra*, what is its antecedent? What is the antecedent for each *ille* in line 8 and the *ille* in line 12?

2. What is the tense, voice and mood for these verb forms?

    habet in line 1

    crēde in line 2

    convenit in line 3

    sequētur in line 10

    exteret in line 12

    quaeret in line 14

3. List the six participles in lines 1–14 and identify the usage of each. Which participle occurs three times? Is it used the same way each time?

4. A contraction or dropping of a syllable such as was noted in line 5's *petiēre* is a poetic figure called SYNCOPE. What is a similar musical phenomenon/term?

5. In lines 10–14, what five actions will the *strenuus amāns* undertake in his pursuit of the *puellam* (line 9)?

6. How many instances of ANAPHORA exist in lines 1–14?

7. Is the phrase *verrendīs aquīs* dative or ablative? What textual evidence supports this reading?

8. The poetic device of APOSTROPHE is the dramatic address of an absent party as if that party were present. How many instances occur in lines 15–32?

9. Are there examples of SYNECDOCHE and METONYMY in lines 15–32? of CHIASMUS and SYNCHESIS?

LITERARY ANALYSIS AND DISCUSSION

1. The confusing personal references in lines 19–20 are artfully designed. Note, for example, the CHIASMUS of *Ille...hic...hic...ille*. The antecedents, however, are in a SYNCHESIS: soldier-lover-soldier-lover. Might this thorough blend highlight the thoroughly blended METAPHOR of the soldier-lover?

2. *Ergō* in line 31 marks the poet's logical conclusion to his contention that "Every lover is a soldier." What is his conclusion?

INTRODUCTION

This Unit Review consists of three sections for each unmodified poem: an introduction, a section addressing textual matters, and some points to ponder. Each introduction contains less emphasis on content summary and a greater focus upon interpretive commentary and literary background. The meter of each poem is identified (see **Appendix 3** for more on Metrics). Each "Textual Matters" section addresses the differences between the modified text (already seen and studied) and the unmodified verse of the original poem. This section also calls attention to the differences between the syntactic phrasing of the modified text and the poetic phrasing of the original. Finally, the "Points to Ponder" questions focus less upon textual analysis and discussion and more upon literary analysis so as to encourage the readers toward a more profound interpretive appreciation of each poem as a whole. At the end of the Unit Review is a brief "Recapitulation" section to help students synthesize their ideas on all three poets.

Cupid

CATULLUS

The Latin text of the Catullus poems is essentially that of F. W. Cornish as revised in 1962 and reprinted in 1976 in the Loeb Classical Library's edition. A few spellings and punctuations have been normalized.

CATULLUS 51 Unmodified

In this poem Catullus uses the same stanzaic format as Sappho, a meter called the Sapphic stanza. Note that line 8 is inside brackets. This is because there was a lacuna (or gap) in the original manuscript at this point. Two earlier German scholars, Ritter and Doring, proposed the words written here, and the square brackets indicate that these words are a suggestion to correct a flaw. Lines 13–16 were not part of Sappho's original (nor were they included in SELECTION I earlier). Some editors think that they are a fragment of a separate poem, while others think they are part of this poem. A translation of these added lines is provided in Points to Ponder, #3. Meter: Sapphic Stanza.

> Ille mī pār esse deō vidētur,
> ille, sī fās est, superāre dīvōs,
> quī sedēns adversus identidem tē
> spectat et audit
>
> 5   dulce rīdentem, miserō quod omnēs
> ēripit sensūs mihi: nam simul tē,
> Lesbia, aspexī, nihil est super mī
> [vōcis in ōre]
>
> lingua sed torpet, tenuis sub artūs
> 10   flamma dēmānat, sonitū suōpte
> tintinant aurēs, geminā teguntur
> lūmina nocte.
>
> Ōtium, Catulle, tibi molestum est;
> ōtiō exsultās nimiumque gestīs.
> 15   Ōtium et regēs prius et beātās
> perdidit urbēs.

TEXTUAL MATTERS

Stanza 1.   Much **ellipsis** occurs in the opening lines.

Stanza 2.   a.   Emphasis on *miserō* is obtained by putting it first in its clause and separating it as far as possible from the word it modifies *(mihi)*. This is a clear example of the important distinction between <u>syntactical</u> phrasing of the sort encountered previously and <u>poetic</u> phrasing of the sort to be experienced regularly in authentic Latin poetry.

         b.   The *atque* after *simul* is omitted, and *est super = superest*.

Stanza 3.   a.   *Tenuis* is in an emphatic position at the beginning of its clause.

         b.   The enclitic *-pte (suōpte)* adds the emphasis of an intensive idea to *suō*: "their very own." cf. Rapid Review #7.

Stanza 4.   a.   *Ōtium* is a word used by Catullus to refer to private as contrasted with public duties. It is not merely idleness or leisure.

         b.   The initial placement of the *ōtium* form in lines 13, 14 and 15 is emphatic.

POINTS TO PONDER

1. If the *Ille* is compared to a god *(par deō)*, in what way(s) might he be "god-like?" What does this implicitly suggest his female companion is? Why might the poet make such a suggestion?

2. In discussing this poem, the commentator Small wrote: "Even though no. 51 may well be his earliest poem to Lesbia, it is not a happy poem." Do you agree or disagree with his assessment of the poem's mood?

3. Here is a literal translation of lines 13–16:

   "Doing your own thing," Catullus, for you is an annoyance (pain):
   in "doing your own thing" you exult and you overly desire it.
   "Doing one's own thing" earlier destroyed kings
   and blessed (well-to-do) cities.

   a.   Some commentators believe that this stanza was added after the affair had ended. If this is the case, what comment on the first three stanzas might Catullus have intended?

   b.   Painful as *ōtium* may be, it is necessary for both love (as in this poem) and poetic creativity. In fact, out of the pain caused to the poet by the sight of Lesbia has come this very poem. Do you agree or disagree with this assessment?

   c.   What is the relevance of the mention of "kings" and "cities" to the plight of the smitten individual?

4. At whom is the poem really directed—the *ille?* Lesbia? Catullus? the reader?

CATULLUS 43 Unmodified

Though the *puella* of this poem is unnamed, she is easily identified by line 5. That line is repeated from Catullus' poem 41, a scandalously explicit poem in which she <u>is</u> identified. Her name seems to have been Ameana, and she seems to have been a readily available and very busy prostitute. More to the point, she was the *amīca*, girlfriend or mistress, of someone detested by Catullus. This "someone" was a man from Formiae in southern Latium whose name was Mamurra. A very successful *praefectus fabrum* ("superintendent of the engineers") for Julius Caesar in Spain and Gaul, he seems to have become very wealthy and a very big spender as well. Calling him *dēcoctor* ("bankrupt") emphasizes his wasteful spending habit. Catullus mentioned or referred to him in nine poems, always unfavorably. Meter: Hendecasyllables.

> Salvē, nec minimō puella nāsō
> nec bellō pede nec nigrīs ocellīs
> nec longīs digitīs nec ōre siccō
> nec sānē nimis ēlegante linguā,
> 5   dēcoctōris amīca Formiānī.
> Tēn Prōvincia narrat esse bellam?
> Tēcum Lesbia nostra comparātur?
> Ō saeclum insapiēns et infacētum!

TEXTUAL MATTERS

1. In this unmodified version, line 1's *puella* is embedded in the descriptive ablative phrase *(nec minimō . . . nasō)* rather than being set off by commas, as it was in the modified version.

2. Line 5 was not included in the modified version (SELECTION II): the *puella* is said to be the *amīca* of the bankrupt guy from Formiae, and ALL of Catullus' readers knew who that had to be. They also knew that there was no way he could literally be bankrupt or spent out, so they recognized the reference as Catullan humor. Some commentators suggest that the term has sexual overtones, that Mamurra had expended all his sexual resources on the *amīca*.

3. *Tēn* in line 6 = *Tēne*.

4. The contracted form *saeclum* in line 8 = *saeculum* by SYNCOPE.

POINTS TO PONDER

1. Do you find *salvē* here friendly or sarcastic?

2. Note the sequence as the poet catalogues Ameana's flaws: physical, social, personal. In light of the focus of the next two lines on Lesbia, what does the poet gain by this sequence?

3. What word picture does line 5 provide?

4. Is there perhaps some social snobbery from the urbane poet in the reference to the *Prōvincia*? What were Catullus' own origins? Might he be stressing how far he himself has come from those origins and how different his acquired tastes have become?

CATULLUS 86 Unmodified

In this poem the beauty of two women, Quintia and Lesbia, is compared. The reader is first introduced to Quintia, her attractions and her merits as *formōsa*. The poet then denies that the collection of individual features qualifies as true *formōsitās*. By way of contrast, the poet then cites Lesbia as an example of true *formōsitās* and describes what makes her genuinely *formōsa*. Meter: Elegiac Couplet.

> Quintia formōsa est multīs; mihi candida, longa,
> recta est. Haec ego sīc singula confiteor,
> tōtum illud formōsa negō: nam nulla venustās,
> nulla in tam magnō est corpore mīca salis.

5   Lesbia formōsa est, quae cum pulcherrima tōta est,
> tum omnibus ūna omnēs surripuit Venerēs.

TEXTUAL MATTERS

1. The *esse formōsum* in the modified version's line 4 reads *formōsa* in line 3 here. The adjective is attracted into agreement with the earlier mentioned Quintia and her adjectives (lines 1–2).

2. In line 4 notice again the agreement between the line's beginning and its ending *(nulla . . . mīca salis)*. Much of Latin poetry does this, so starting to anticipate it will improve reading skill a great deal. Cf. the typical placement of subject and verb in a Latin prose sentence.

3. The *cum . . . tum* correlative pair in lines 5–6 here replaces the more commonly seen *et . . . et* which was substituted in the modified version. Each pair means the same thing (cf. Rapid Review #3).

4. In similar fashion the *sōla* in the modified version's line 6 has been replaced by *ūna* here.

5. Notice that *Venerēs* receives a double emphasis: last word of its line and of the poem.

POINTS TO PONDER

1. How many different contrasts are to be found in this short poem? Which ones are emphasized more than others? How does the poet attain this emphasis?

2. What provides the humor in line 4?

3. Did Catullus consider *formōsa* and *pulcherrima* to have contrasting or parallel meanings? With which term is *venustās* associated?

CATULLUS 5 Unmodified

This poem reflects the spontaneity and passion characteristic of Catullus early in his relationship with Lesbia. The opening sentence introduces three main themes, each of which is explored more fully in the remainder of the poem. These themes—living life to the fullest, loving, and deflecting the envy of others—represent common topics often explored by ancient poets. Meter: Hendecasyllables.

> Vīvāmus, mea Lesbia, atque amēmus,
> rūmōrēsque senum sevēriōrum
> omnēs ūnīus aestimēmus assis!
> Sōlēs occidere et redīre possunt:
> 5 nōbīs cum semel occidit brevis lux,
> nox est perpetua ūna dormienda.
> Da mī bāsia mille, deinde centum,
> dein mille altera, dein secunda centum,
> deinde usque altera mille, deinde centum.
> 10 Dein, cum mīlia multa fēcerīmus,
> conturbābimus illa, nē sciāmus,
> aut nē quis malus invidēre possit,
> cum tantum sciat esse bāsiōrum.

TEXTUAL MATTERS

1. In line 3, the separation of *omnēs* from its noun enables the juxtaposition of *omnēs* to *ūnīus*.

2. *Redīre* in line 4 has replaced the modified version's *resurgere*.

3. In lines 5–6 the reversed order of *occidit* and *brevis lux* enables the striking contrast of *lux* and *nox* to be highlighted.

4. Line 13's compactly colloquial phrase *tantum basiōrum* here replaces the more prosaic and formal *tantum . . . numerum bāsiōrum* seen in the earlier modified version.

POINTS TO PONDER

1. Look carefully at line 1. How does the word order clarify the poet's central focus of living and loving?

2. The commentator J. Ferguson notes the careful balance of the opening triads: lines 1–3 start with the lovers (*vīvāmus . . . amēmus*) and end with the little circle of an almost worthless coin (*assis*), while lines 4–6 start with the great circle of the sun (*sōlēs*) and end with the lovers reduced to the nothingness of death's eternal sleep (*dormienda*). Are there other instances of tight artistic control in a poem about completely "letting go?"

3. What do the large numbers of kisses in lines 7–10 suggest about the poet's passion? How is this "large number of kisses" related to the poem's third theme?

CATULLUS 70 Unmodified

This poem's themes are the proverbial mutability of a woman and her evasiveness when pursued. It emphasizes the untrustworthy nature of words uttered in the heat of passion and culminates in an image both proverbial and striking. Meter: Elegiac Couplet.

Nullī sē dīcit mulier mea nūbere malle
    quam mihi, nōn sī sē Iuppiter ipse petat.
Dīcit: sed mulier cupidō quod dīcit amantī
    in ventō et rapidā scrībere oportet aquā.

TEXTUAL MATTERS

1. In lines 1–2, the first word–last word arrangement of *Nullī . . . mihi* makes an emphatic contrast.

2. In lines 3–4, the placement of *mulier* and *aquā* adds emphasis to the two nouns.

POINTS TO PONDER

1. *Mulier* is an ordinary word for "woman," while *fēmina* often has a more complimentary tone to it, akin perhaps to our "lady." What may be an implication of the distinction for this poem?

2. Why is the *mulier* in line 3 lacking a modifying *mea* (cf. line 1)? Who <u>is</u> the *mulier* of line 3? Who is the *amantī*?

3. How does the poet emphasize the impermanence of line 4's "wind and water?"

4. *Dīcit* is a key word in the poem. How does the poet make this point unmistakable? What does the poet gain by the change from the emphatic *dīcit* to *scrībere* for the concluding image?

5. What is the poet's tone or mood as he describes his distrust of a woman's words?

CATULLUS 8 Unmodified

Lesbia seems to have broken off her relationship with Catullus, and in reaction he penned this poem of renunciation. He addresses himself, briefly recalls the affair's course and urges himself to remain firm in his resolve despite feeling sorry for himself. The poem provides an insightful study of the struggle between the emotional and rational sides of someone's personality. Earlier you read lines 12–18; a literal translation of lines 1–11 follows to provide the context and set the stage for a review of the lines studied previously. Meter: Choliambic (Limping Iambic, Scazon).

> Miserable Catullus, you should stop being a fool,
> and that which you see to have perished you should consider destroyed.
> Formerly suns shone bright for you,
> when you always used to come where the girl was leading,
> loved by us as much as not any will be loved.
> Then, when those many jolly times used to happen
> which you were wanting nor was that girl not wanting,
> suns shone truly bright for you.
> Now that girl no longer is willing; you too, powerless one, be unwilling,
> and do not keep following after one who flees, and do not live miserable,
> but stick it out with resolute mind, be firm.

Miser Catulle, dēsinās ineptīre,
et quod vidēs perīsse perditum dūcās.
Fulsēre quondam candidī tibi sōlēs,
cum ventitābās quō puella dūcēbat
5   amāta nōbīs quantum amābitur nulla.
Ibi illa multa tum iocōsa fīēbant,
quae tū volēbās nec puella nōlēbat.
Fulsēre vērē candidī tibi sōlēs.
Nunc iam illa nōn volt: tū quoque impotēns [nōlī],
10   nec quae fugit sectāre, nec miser vīve,
<u>sed obstinātā mente perfer, obdūrā.</u>
Valē, puella. Iam Catullus obdūrat,
nec tē requīret nec rogābit invītam:
at tū dolēbis, cum rogāberis nulla.
15   Scelesta, vae tē. Quae tibi manet vīta?
Quis nunc tē adībit? Cui vidēberis bella?
Quem nunc amābis? Cūius esse dīcēris?
Quem bāsiābis? Cui labella mordēbis?
At tū, Catulle, dēstinātus obdūrā.

TEXTUAL MATTERS

1. *volt* in line 9 is a variant for *vult*.

2. There is an ELLIPSIS of *tē* in the second half of line 13.

3. Line 14 reads *nulla* here rather than the earlier version's *nihil*, and *nulla* gains emphasis from its final position in its line.

4. In line 18, the dative *cui* appears where the earlier version had the genitive *cūius*.

POINTS TO PONDER

1. Why does Catullus name himself but not his lover? Why is it significant that the usual *mea* with *puella* is lacking?

2. The technique of self-address is familiar from epic and drama, but Catullus seems the first to employ it in personal poetry. What does he gain by using this technique?

3. Daniel Garrison suggests that *scelesta* contains the ideas of "scorn and pity," while P. Forsyth suggests the meaning of "unlucky" and O. Lyne "unfortunate" due to the misery awaiting her from his resolve to remain firm. Which suggestion is most appropriate? Why?

4. The poem begins with Catullus giving himself polite commands in jussive subjunctives (*dēsinās* and *dūcās*) and ends with him addressing himself with the direct command of an imperative (*obdūrā*). What accounts for the change?

HORACE

The Latin text of Horace's *Odes* is essentially that of C. E. Bennett as revised in 1927 and reprinted in 1968 in the Loeb Classical Library's edition. A few spellings and punctuations have been normalized.

Horace *Odes* I.23 Unmodified

In his poetry, Horace often uses images from the cycle of nature to represent aspects of the human life cycle. Chloe is a young maiden on the cusp (brink/edge) of entering womanhood. In this poem, Horace tries to demonstrate that her fears are as baseless as those of the fawn to whom she is compared. Meter: Fourth Asclepiadean Stanza.

>Vītās innuleō mē similis, Chloē,
>quaerentī pavidam montibus āviīs
>   matrem nōn sine vānō
>   aurārum et silvae metū.

5
>Nam seu mōbilibus vēris inhorruit
>adventus foliīs, seu viridēs rubum
>   dīmōvēre lacertae,
>   et corde et genibus tremit.

>Atquī nōn ego tē tigris ut aspera
10
>Gaetūlusve leō frangere persequor:
>   tandem dēsine matrem
>   tempestīva sequī virō.

TEXTUAL MATTERS

Note the prominent ENJAMBMENT: lines 1–4, 5–7, 9–10 and 11–12.

Stanza 1	Due to the separation of the adjectives *quaerentī, pavidam* and *vānō* from their nouns, it is important to read and reread the stanza until the thought groups are clear and the poetic phrasing is apparent.
Stanza 2	The first word–last word (in a phrase/clause) modification arrangements in *mōbilibus...foliīs* and in *viridēs...lacertae* are typical.
Stanza 3	In lines 9–10, the main idea's completion is delayed by the placement of the simile (*tigris . . . leo*). In lines 11–12, notice that the *matrem* and daughter (described as *tempestīva*) remain side by side linearly though they are not visually.

POINTS TO PONDER

1. The fawn's mother is described as *pavidam* (line 2). What does this tell the reader about <u>Chloe</u>?

2. In the last stanza, what two reasons does the poet provide to convince Chloe that her fears of him are unfounded?

3. Despite the literal denial in the words' <u>meanings</u>, the <u>imagery</u> of lines 9–10 is filled with ideas of force, aggression and blood. What connection exists between this imagery and the phrase *tempestīva . . . virō*?

Horace *Odes* III.9 Unmodified

This poem consists of a conversation between two lovers, a man and a woman. It exemplifies a very specific
type of poetic genre known as *carmen amoebaeum,* or amoebean song. In all amoebean song, there is an element
of competition, wherein the second speaker should reply to the first in similar verse and subject matter, but
"cap" him with superior artistry of expression. Its roots lie in the Greek poetry of Theocritus and, in addition
to Horace, there are examples in both Vergil (*Eclogues* 3 and 7) and Catullus (poems 45 and 62). Some scholars
identify the man in this dialogue as Horace, though the elements that would support or refute this supposition
remain ambiguous. Meter: Second Asclepiadean Stanza.

"Dōnec grātus eram tibi
    nec quisquam potior bracchia candidae
cervīcī iuvenis dabat,
    Persārum viguī rēge beātior."

5   "Dōnec nōn aliā magis
    arsistī neque erat Lȳdia post Chloēn,
multī Lȳdia nōminis
    Rōmānā viguī clārior Īliā."

"Mē nunc Thressa Chloē regit,
10   dulcēs docta modōs et citharae sciēns,
prō quā nōn metuam morī,
    sī parcent animae fāta superstitī."

"Mē torret face mūtuā
    Thūrīnī Calais fīlius Ornytī,
15   prō quō bis patiar morī,
    sī parcent puerō fāta superstitī."

"Quid sī prisca redit Venus
    dīductōsque iugō cōgit aēneō?
Sī flāva excutitur Chloē
20   reiectaeque patet iānua Lȳdiae?"

"Quamquam sīdere pulchrior
    ille est, tū levior cortice et improbō
īrācundior Hadriā,
    tēcum vīvere amem, tēcum obeam libēns!"

TEXTUAL MATTERS

Stanzas 1–2   An embracing effect is attained by the **HYPERBATON** *quisquam potior...iuvenis.* The verbal picture of an intertwined couple continues in line 4's **SYNCHESIS**.

Stanzas 3–4   The emphatically positioned *mē* begins each stanza. Lȳdia delays naming her new man until after his effect on her has been stressed in line 13.

Stanzas 5–6   The idea of union found in *iugō* is reinforced by line 18's **SYNCHESIS**; note also the now familiar first word–last word agreement in line 20.

POINTS TO PONDER

1. Line 2's *potior* suggests that while they were still together there were other men in her life but that he was the one she really preferred. Is such an insinuation meant to "needle" her?

2. What "needle" in Lȳdia's response in lines 5–8 answers his? How does her reference to "Roman Ilia" outdo his to the "ruler of the Persians?"

3. In lines 9–12 the man seems to be making three points:

    a.   he has a new lover;

    b.   she is accomplished artistically;

    c.   he is ready to die for Chloe.

    In lines 13–16 she then caps each of these points:

    a.   her new love is <u>mutual</u>. What is the implication for his love?

    b.   her new Calais is from a respectable Italian family. What is the implication for his Chloe?

    c.   she also is ready to die for Calais. How is her statement stronger than his?

4. In lines 17–20, what does the phrase *iugum aēneum* symbolize about his proposal-the yoke of love or of subjugation?

5. Who in your view "wins" the contest?

Horace *Odes* III.26 Unmodified

In this poem, Horace apparently is retiring from the battlefield of love, and he therefore dedicates his weaponry to Venus and offers a prayer to her. The metaphor of love as war is common among Greek and Roman authors. Additionally, this poem combines two traditional types of ancient poetry. First, it appears to be a dedicatory piece, in which the speaker (usually a craftsman, a fisherman, a soldier, etc.), upon retirement, dedicates the tools of his trade to the gods and expresses thanks for the successes he has had as a result of their kindness. Second, the poem can also be seen as a prayer, in which the speaker, by naming and renaming the god and her dwelling places, and by dedicating his tools to the deity, asks for even greater success in his field. Hence Horace may be asking Venus to influence Chloe, thereby affording him one more chance with Chloe. Meter: Alcaic Stanza.

> Vīxī puellīs nūper idōneus
> et mīlitāvī nōn sine glōriā;
> nunc arma dēfunctumque bellō
> barbiton hic pariēs habēbit,

5   laevum marīnae quī Veneris latus
> custōdit. Hīc, hīc pōnite lūcida
> fūnālia et vectēs et arcūs
> oppositīs foribus mināces.

> Ō quae beātam dīva tenēs Cyprum et
10 Memphin carentem Sīthoniā nive,
> rēgīna, sublīmī flagellō
> tange Chloēn semel arrogantem.

TEXTUAL MATTERS

Stanza 1   Notice that the subject for lines 3–4 is delayed until after the objects have been mentioned.

Stanza 2   Line 5 is arranged in a **CHIASTIC** word order: ABCBA.

Stanza 3   Note that the vocative *dīva* is delayed and embedded in the following relative clause, and that a second *Ō* for *rēgīna* is **ELLIPSED.**

POINTS TO PONDER

1. In whose "army" has the poet been a "soldier?"

2. What is the implication of the fact that the torches (line 7) are described as *lūcida*-still aflame?

3. The plea to queen Venus to discipline her "disobedient subject" Chloe so that she'll regret her hardheartedness recalls Catullus 8's *At tū dolēbis* . . . What similarities/differences exist between the two poems and their situations? Which poem is more effective? Why?

OVID

The Latin text of Ovid's *Amōrēs* is essentially that of Grant Showerman as reprinted in 1958 in the Loeb Classical Library's edition. A few spellings and punctuations have been normalized.

Ovid *Amōrēs* I.5 Unmodified

In this poem, Ovid reflects upon a pleasant afternoon spent in the company of his lover, Corinna. Ovid's detailed description of the quality of the light serves as an anticipatory prelude to his reminiscence. Meter: Elegiac Couplet.

Aestus erat, mediamque diēs exēgerat hōram;
    adposuī mediō membra levanda torō.
Pars adaperta fuit, pars altera clausa fenestrae;
    quāle ferē silvae lūmen habēre solent,
5   quālia sublūcent fugiente crepuscula Phoebō,
    aut ubi nox abiit, nec tamen orta diēs.
Illa verēcundīs lux est praebenda puellīs,
    quā timidus latebrās spēret habēre pudor.
Ecce, Corinna venit, tunicā vēlāta recinctā,
10   candida dīviduā colla tegente comā —
quāliter in thalamōs fāmōsa Semīramis īsse
    dīcitur, et multīs Lāis amāta virīs.
Dēripuī tunicam — nec multum rāra nocēbat;
    pugnābat tunicā sed tamen illa tegī.
15 Quae cum ita pugnāret, tamquam quae vincere nollet,
    victa est nōn aegrē prōditiōne suā.
Ut stetit ante oculōs positō vēlāmine nostrōs,
    in tōtō nusquam corpore menda fuit.
    . . . .
20   . . . .
    . . . .
    . . . .
Singula quid referam? Nil nōn laudābile vīdī
    et nūdam pressī corpus ad usque meum.
25 Cētera quis nescit? Lassī requiēvimus ambō.
    Prōveniant mediī sīc mihi saepe diēs!

TEXTUAL MATTERS

1. Note the now familiar first word–last word arrangement in line 1.

2. In line 3 there is an ELLIPSIS of *fenestrae* with the initial *pars,* and of *fuit* with *clausa.*

3. In lines 5–8, the adjectives *quālia, verēcundīs* and *timidus* are separated from their nouns.

4. In lines 9–10 be sure to pay attention to the difference in the -a endings.

5. In line 14 note the delayed position of the phrase *sed tamen illa.*

6. *Nostrōs* is separated from *oculōs* in line 17.

7. In line 24 *ad usque* = *usque ad.*

8. Line 26 illustrates both the separation of *mediī* from its noun *diēs* and the familiar first word–last word arrangement.

POINTS TO PONDER

1. What adjective most fittingly describes this poem—playful? tender? sensuous?

2. The events of the poem are told from his point of view. Is Corinna's perspective represented at all?

3. Was the visit pre-arranged or unexpected? Is it significant that <u>she</u> came to <u>his</u> residence?

4. Explain the irony in the phrases *verēcundīs . . . puellīs* and *timidus . . . pudor* in lines 7–8.

Ovid *Amōrēs* I.9.1–32 Unmodified

In this poem the reader is to imagine that someone named Atticus has criticized the poet for a life of leisured laziness and unproductivity. The poet disagrees, claiming in an extended metaphor that an able lover must be as fit as any soldier. His preparations are as demanding, his battles as challenging and his victories as glorious. To prove his point, he concludes with three mythological *exampla* of famous warrior-lovers: Achilles, Hector and Mars himself. The conclusion, lines 33–46, is translated below the Latin text. Meter: Elegiac couplet.

      Mīlitat omnis amāns, et habet sua castra Cupīdō;
          Attice, crēde mihi, mīlitat omnis amāns.
      Quae bellō est habilis, Venerī quoque convenit aetās.
          Turpe senex mīles, turpe senīlis amor.
5   Quōs petiēre ducēs animōs in mīlite fortī,
          hōs petit in sociō bella puella virō:
      pervigilant ambō; terrā requiescit uterque—
          ille forēs dominae servat, at ille ducis.
      Mīlitis officium longa est via; mitte puellam,
10   strenuus exemptō fīne sequētur amāns.
      Ībit in adversōs montēs duplicātaque nimbō
          flūmina, congestās exteret ille nivēs,
      nec freta pressūrus tumidōs causābitur Eurōs
          aptaque verrendīs sīdera quaeret aquīs.
15   Quis nisi vel mīles vel amāns et frīgora noctis
          et densō mixtās perferet imbre nivēs?
      Mittitur infestōs alter speculātor in hostēs;
          in rīvāle oculōs alter, ut hoste, tenet.
      Ille gravēs urbēs, hic dūrae līmen amīcae
20   obsidet; hic portās frangit, at ille forēs.
      Saepe sopōrātōs invādere profuit hostēs
          caedere et armātā vulgus inerme manū.
      Sīc fera Thrēiciī cecidērunt agmina Rhēsī,
          et dominum captī dēseruistis equī.
25   Nempe marītōrum somnīs ūtuntur amantēs,
          et sua sōpītīs hostibus arma movent.
      Custōdum transīre manūs vigilumque catervās
          mīlitis et miserī semper amantis opus.
      Mars dubius nec certa Venus; victīque resurgunt,
30   quōsque negēs umquam posse iacēre, cadunt.

Ergō dēsidiam quīcumque vocābat amōrem,
   dēsinat. Ingeniī est experientis Amor.

. . . .

Ardet in abductā Brīsēide magnus Achillēs —
   dum licet, Argīvās frangite, Trōes, opēs!
35 Hector ab Andromachēs complexibus ībat ad arma,
   et, galeam capitī quae daret, uxor erat.
Summa ducum, Atrīdēs, vīsā Priamēide fertur
   Maenadis effūsīs obstipuisse comīs.
Mars quoque dēprēnsus fabrīlia vincula sēnsit;
40 nōtior in caelō fābula nulla fuit.
Ipse ego segnis eram discinctaque in ōtia nātus;
   mollierant animōs lectus et umbra meōs.
Impulit ignāvum formōsae cūra puellae
   iussit et in castrīs aera merēre suīs.
45 Inde vidēs agilem nocturnaque bella gerentem.
   Quī nōlet fierī dēsidiōsus, amet!

Translation of Lines 33–46

> Great Achilles was on fire for Briseis who had been taken away [by Agamemnon] —
> break the Greek defenses while it's allowed, Trojans!
> Hector went to arms from Andromache's embraces
> and his wife was the one to give him his helmet for his head.
> Atreus' son [Agamemnon], the greatest of generals, is said to have been astounded
> when Priam's daughter [Cassandra] was seen with the disheveled hair of a Bacchante.
> Mars also was caught and felt the chains forged [by Vulcan];
> no tale was more familiar in heaven.
> I myself was slack and born for undisciplined leisure;
> my shady couch had softened my spirit;
> Love for a shapely girl drove me from my laziness
> and ordered me to earn my wages in its camp.
> From this you see me active and waging the wars of the night.
> Whoever won't want to become lazy-let him be a lover.

TEXTUAL MATTERS

1. The postponed position of *Cupīdō* to the end of line 1 adds emphasis.
2. The postponed positioning of *aetās* in line 3 produces a typical first word–last word arrangement.
3. In line 6, the delayed subject *bella puella* interrupts the ablative phrase *in sociō . . . virō.*
4. Line 10 illustrates a typical first word–last word arrangement.
5. In line 12, there is a variation on the first word–last word scheme: here it is limited to the second clause.
6. Though the modified text's line 14 was introduced by *aut*, it is replaced here by the enclitic *-que*. Note too that a SYNCHESIS both in line 14 and in line 16 is interrupted by a verb.
7. In line 17, *infestōs* is separated from its noun *hostēs.*
8. In lines 17–18, each *alter* is delayed until after an accusative case word, and in line 22, the *et* is delayed until after *caedere.*
9. Line 24 exemplifies both the separation of *captī* from its noun *equī* and that the separation provides an internal rhyme between the line's middle and its end.

POINTS TO PONDER

1. Who in this poem is the lover/warrior's commanding officer? Who was it in *Ode* III.26? Is the difference significant?
2. When a lover is a "warrior," whom is he seeking to "overcome"—the girl? a rival? his own overwhelming feelings (and hence himself)?
3. In considering *Ode* III.26 and this poem of similar theme, what are the similarities and differences? Which poem presents its case more effectively? How does it do so?

RECAPITULATION

In the poems included in this unit, you have entered the inner worlds of three great poets. Their greatness is assured, for their works have been appreciated by successive generations and have continued to influence other poets. Though they lived long ago, their humanness and ours have much in common. They have willingly shared the sometime rocky road of their romances, and you have been part of their agonies and their ecstasies, their laughter and their tears.

1. What has been each poet's attitude toward love and toward his lover?
2. Several women have appeared in the poems: Lesbia, Ameana and Quintia in Catullus; Chloe and Lȳdia in Horace; Corinna in Ovid.
    a. What are their similarities and differences?
    b. What does each poet value the most in a woman?
3. For Catullus love was life; for Horace love was a memory; and for Ovid love was an amusing game. What is your assessment of this statement?
4. With which poet do you most identify? Why?

APPENDIX A: TIMELINES FOR CATULLUS, HORACE AND OVID

Decade	Date	Catullus	Horace	Ovid
90 BCE*				
	85/84	C.'s birth		
80 BCE				
70 BCE				
	65		H.'s birth	
	62	C. in Rome		
	61	C. meets Clodia		
60 BCE				
	58	C. in Bithynia		
	54	C. dies		
50 BCE				
	46/45		H. to Greece	
	43			O.'s birth
	42		Battle of Philippi	
	41		H. back to Rome	
40 BCE				
	39		H. introduced to Maecenas	
	33		H. gets farm	
	31		Battle of Actium	
30 BCE				
	24/23			O. rejects politics, publishes *Amores*
	23		*Odes* I—III published	
	late 20s			O. in Rome, Athens, Sicily and Rome
20 BCE				
10 BCE				
	8		H. dies	
CE* starts				
	8			O. banished to Tomis
10 CE				
	14			death of Augustus
	17			O. dies
20 CE				

APPENDIX B: POETIC DEVICES/LITERARY TERMS

The following is a listing of terms used in this *Libellus*. Parenthetical citations indicate where the device is introduced.

ALLITERATION: the repetition of the same initial sound, generally a consonant, at the beginning of two or more words.

> **Example:** s̲enum s̲evēriōrum (SELECTION IV)

ANAPHORA: the repetition of a word with the same or different inflection at the beginning of successive phrases, clauses or stanzas.

> **Example:** n̲e̲c̲ . . . n̲e̲c̲ . . . n̲e̲c̲ . . . n̲e̲c̲ . . . n̲e̲c̲ . . . (SELECTION II)

APOSTROPHE: the dramatic "turning away" to address an absent party as if that party were present.

> **Example:** dominum deseruistis, c̲a̲p̲t̲ī̲ e̲q̲u̲ī̲. (SELECTION XI-B)

ASSONANCE: the close repetition of similar sounds, generally vowels, usually at the middle or end of words.

> **Example:** me̲a Lesbi̲a̲ (SELECTION IV)

ASYNDETON: the omission of a conjunction between words, phrases, clauses or sentences.

> **Example:** candida, longa, recta est (SELECTION III)

CHIASMUS: a word order arrangement in which the words are arranged in a "bookend" or ABBA order. Chiasmus may occur with words, inflectional forms, parts of speech, phrases or ideas. Cf. **SYNCHESIS** below.

> **Example:** laevum (accus.) marīnae (gen.) Veneris (gen.) latus (accus.) (SELECTION IX)

ELLIPSIS: the omission of a word or words easily inferred from the context.

> **Example:** Tū (e̲s̲) levior cortice (SELECTION VIII-B)

ENJAMBMENT (run-on line): the running-on from one line (or stanza) to the next calls attention to that part which runs on.

> **Example:** ībit in adversōs montēs duplicātaque nimbō/flūmina, . . . (INTRODUCTION TO OVID)

FRAMING: an arrangement of words that also pictures their meaning. Some prefer to call such an arrangement a "word picture," using "framing" more narrowly to describe a line of verse enclosed by two closely connected words, e.g. a noun and its adjective, at line beginning and line end.

> **Example:** . . . m̲e̲d̲i̲ō̲ membra levanda t̲o̲r̲ō̲ where the limbs are in the middle of the bed (SELECTION X-B)

HYPERBATON: the wide separation of a noun and its modifying adjective.

> **Example:** Nam seu m̲ō̲b̲i̲l̲i̲b̲u̲s̲ vēris inhorruit/adventus f̲o̲l̲i̲ī̲s̲, . . . (INTRODUCTION TO HORACE)

HYPERBOLE: the use of exaggeration or overstatement to heighten the dramatic effect of the description.

> **Example:** basia mille, deinde centum (SELECTION I)

IRONY: using words whose implied meaning differs from their explicit meaning so as to produce humor, ridicule, or gentle sarcasm. It can involve statements, events or situations.

> **Example:** Jupiter as a potential marriage partner (SELECTION V)

LITOTES: the practice of asserting something by denying its opposite or by understatement.

> **Example:** nōn sine in place of *cum* (SELECTION VII)

METAPHOR: a form of comparison that uses a word or phrase to imply a likeness between what is described and something else.

> **Example:** nox . . . perpetua for death (SELECTION IV)

METONYMY: the substitution of one word for another closely related to it.

> **Example:** lūmina for "eyes" (SELECTION I)

SYNCHESIS (SYNCHYSIS): a word order in which the agreeing words are interlocked in an ABAB arrangement.

> **Example:** Lāis multīs amāta virīs
> Contrast this arrangement with **chiasmus** and its ABBA order. (SELECTION X-A)

SYNCOPE: the shortening of a word by contracting or dropping a syllable.

> **Example:** petiēre for *petīvērunt* (SELECTION XI-B)

SYNECDOCHE: using a part to stand for (or represent) a whole.

> **Example:** using membra to stand for the entire body (*corpus*) (SELECTION X-B)

APPENDIX C: METRICS

In many languages, poetry focuses not so much on content as on the way in which that content is conveyed through sounds, images, symbols and rhythm. Poetry expresses emotions and opens a window into the author's soul. Hence, there is a very special and close relationship between a poet and his audience, for the poet is directing his efforts at their hearts as well as their minds. One way a poet achieves this aim is through his "music," the rhythm or metrical pattern of his poem. Classical poetry was meant to be heard, not merely read, by its audience. Classical **love** poetry, belonging to the genre of lyric poetry, was meant to be sung to the accompaniment of a lyre.

Obviously, an introductory *libellus* is not intended to provide a complete discussion of this topic. It does, however, provide some examples from three great Roman love poets, offer acquaintance with some basic terms and concepts involved in metrics, and describe various metrical patterns employed by these poets in the SELECTIONS included in it.

In Latin, the meter of a poem is made up of various patterns of rhythm combined into sequences. The basic unit is a metrical **foot** with a specific pattern of long and/or short **syllables** (see the next paragraph for more information on long and short syllables). These syllables are marked by a — over a long syllable and by a ∪ over a short syllable. Some syllables can be either long **or** short; such a syllable is called *anceps* ("two-headed") and marked with an ×. The common metrical "feet" are the **dactyl** (– ∪ ∪), the **spondee** (– –), the **iamb** (∪ –), the **trochee** (– ∪) and the **choriamb** (– ∪ ∪ –). The various patterns into which these metrical "feet" are arranged make up the various poetic meters.

Since Latin meter is based upon long and short **syllables**, there are specific rules to determine the length of a syllable. A **long** syllable is one that:

a. contains a naturally long vowel (like the –ā- in *portāre*) or

b. contains a dipthong (ae, oe, ei, ui, au, eu as in *praeda, proelium,* etc.) or

c. contains a naturally short vowel followed by two or more consonants (like the first syllable in *portāre*).

All other syllables are **short** (the few exceptions to the above statements are beyond the scope of this transitional *libellus*). The final syllable in a line of verse is **always** considered *anceps*. To **scan** a line of poetry is to mark its **long** and **short** syllables.

Three additional important metrical concepts are **elision, caesura** and **diaeresis**. When a word's final syllable is a vowel or dipthong, alone or followed by an –m, and the next word starts with a vowel or dipthong, alone or preceded by an –h, the final syllable is **elided** (from *elīdere* – to strike out): *Ōd(ī)et amō.* Most lines have a brief pause, called a **caesura** (from *caedere* - to "cut"), a break between words **inside** a metrical foot; it is marked by a //. When the break or pause falls not inside the metrical foot but at its end, the pause is called a **diaeresis**, also marked by a //.

METERS OF THE POEMS

The following meters are found in this *libellus*:

> Catullus: Elegiac Couplet, Hendecasyllabic, Sapphic Stanza and the Choliambic also called the Limping Iambic or Scazon

> Horace: Alcaic Stanza, 2nd Asclepiadean Stanza, 4th Asclepiadean Stanza

> Ovid: Elegiac Couplet

An **ELEGIAC COUPLET** has alternating lines of dactylic hexameter (*hex* means "six" in Greek), the standard meter for epic poetry, and dactylic pentameter (*penta* means "five" in Greek). The hexameter line has the following pattern: – ⏑⏑ / – ⏑⏑ / – ⏑⏑ / – ⏑⏑ / – ⏑⏑ / – × . Note the possible variations in the first five feet. The main **caesura** normally occurs after the first syllable in the third or fourth foot. The pentameter is actually 2 ½ feet repeated, with a **diaeresis** between the two parts: – ⏑⏑ / – ⏑⏑ / — // – ∪∪ / – ∪∪ / – . The pair of lines makes up an **elegiac couplet**:

> – ⏑⏑ / – ⏑⏑ / – ⏑⏑ / – ⏑⏑ / – ⏑⏑ / – ×
> – ⏑⏑ / – ⏑⏑ / — // – ∪∪ / – ∪∪ / –

The **HENDECASYLLABIC** is a metrical line that has eleven (*hendeca* in Greek means "eleven") syllables. Note that this time variations are possible only in the first foot.

> ∪̲ ∪̄ / – ∪∪ / – ∪ / – ∪ / – ×

The **SAPPHIC STANZA** (or **STROPHE**) consists of four lines and is named for the Greek female poet Sappho who employed this pattern in her poetry. Note that the fourth syllable in the first three lines may be short. The **caesaura** or **diaeresis** usually (but by no means always) occurs after the fifth syllable. The first three lines are the same, with the fourth line indented.

> – ∪ / – ∪̲ / – // ∪∪ / – ∪ / – ×
> – ∪ / – ∪̲ / – // ∪∪ / – ∪ / – ×
> – ∪ / – ∪̲ / – // ∪∪ / – ∪ / – ×
> – ∪∪ / – ×

The **CHOLIAMBIC** (**LIMPING IAMBIC** or **SCAZON**) line has five iambs followed by a trochee/spondee. A spondee may be substituted in the first and/or third foot. The "limping" quality arises from the abrupt change to a long syllable to begin the final foot.

> ∪̄ – / ∪ – / ∪̄ – / ∪ – / ∪ – / – ×

The **ALCAIC STANZA** (or **STROPHE**) is a favorite Horatian meter and is named after Alcaeus, like Sappho a lyric poet from the island of Lesbos in the Aegean Sea. It looks different from the Sapphic, also a four line stanza, in that only the first two lines are the same, the third line is indented and the fourth line is doubly indented. A **diaeresis** normally occurs after the fifth syllable in the first two lines. The opening syllable in the first three lines is an **anacrusis** ("pick-up beat"), and may be either long or short, though the long is much more common.

> ∪̲ / – ∪ / – – // – ∪∪ / – ∪ ×
> ∪̲ / – ∪ / – – // – ∪∪ / – ∪ ×
> ∪̲ / – ∪ / – – / – ∪ / – ×
> – ∪∪ / – ∪∪ / – ∪ / – ×

There are five **ASCLEPIADEAN** meters, named after the Hellenistic Greek poet Asclepiades who revived the use of these forms used earlier by Sappho and Alcaeus. The **SECOND ASCLEPIADEAN STANZA** alternates two lines (note that the second is indented), and the **diaeresis** is regularly after the sixth syllable in the even numbered lines.

    – – / – ∪ ∪ / – ∪ ×
        – – / – ∪ ∪ – // – ∪ ∪ / – ∪ ×

The **FOURTH ASCLEPIADEAN STANZA** also has four lines but is configured a bit differently. The first two lines are like the even numbered lines in the Second Asclepiadean Stanza, the third line is indented and the fourth is doubly indented (cf. the Alcaic Stanza above).

    – – / – ∪ ∪ – // – ∪ ∪ / – ∪ ×
    – – / – ∪ ∪ – // – ∪ ∪ / – ∪ ×
        – – / – ∪ ∪ / – ×
            – – / – ∪ ∪ / – ∪ ×

*APPENDIX D: LATIN GRAMMAR AND SYNTAX**

Section 1: Declensions of Nouns

Nouns are the names of persons, places, or things. In Latin, nouns, pronouns, and adjectives are inflected to show their grammatical relations to the other words in the sentence. These inflectional endings are sometimes equivalent to prepositional phrases in English.

The names of the cases and their functions are as follows:

Latin Case	Use in the Sentence	English Case	Example
Nominative	Subject or subj. complement.	Nominative.	puer (*the* or *a boy*)
Genitive	Shows possession and other relationships.	Possessive or the objective, with "of."	puerī (*of the boy,* or *of a boy or boy's*)
Dative	Indirect object and other relationships.	Objective, often with "to" or "for."	puerō (*to* or *for the boy*)
Accusative	Direct object.	Objective.	puerum (*boy,* or *the boy*)
Ablative	Occurs in adverbial phrases, usually with a preposition.	Objective, as object of many prepositions.	puerō (*by the boy, from, with, on, at,* etc.)

There are two additional cases which occur infrequently, and are not usually given with the decensions:

Vocative	Case of address. (The Latin inflectional ending is the same as in the nominative with exceptions noted in Rapid Review #2.)	Nominative of address.	puer! *(Boy!)*
Locative	Case of "place at which," with cities, towns, small islands, and **domus** *(home),* and **rūs** (country) only.	Objective, with "at."	Rōmae *(at Rome)*

INFLECTION IN GENERAL

The inflectional ending of a noun, pronoun, or adjective shows its *case, number,* and *gender.* The general concepts of number and case are similar to their counterparts in English (singular-plural, case structure outlined above). However, *gender* in Latin is often *grammatical* only, and unrelated to *natural* gender. Although there are the same three genders (masculine, feminine, neuter) in Latin as in English, it is not uncommon for a word like **nauta** *(sailor),* which is naturally male, to appear in a feminine declension (1st declension). Inflected words are composed of two parts: the *base* and the inflected portion. The *base* is that part of the word which remains unchanged, and the base of any noun may be determined by removing the ending of the *genitive singular* form. The base of **terra, terrae** is **terr-;** the base of **ager, agrī** is **agr-,** and so on.

FIRST AND SECOND DECLENSION NOUNS

The gender of most 1st declension nouns is feminine. That of most 2nd declension nouns is masculine (ending in **-us** or **-er**) or neuter (ending in **-um**).

1st Declension — Fem.

	Sing.	Plur.
Nom.	terra *(land)*	-ae
Gen.	terrae	-ārum
Dat.	terrae	-īs
Acc.	terram	-ās
Abl.	terrā	-īs

	2nd Declension — Masc.		2nd Declension Masc. Ending in -er				2nd Declension — Neut.	
	Sing.	Plur.	Sing.	Plur.	Sing.	Plur.	Sing.	Plur.
Nom.	animus *(mind)*	-ī	magister *(teacher)*	-ī	puer *(boy)*	-ī	caelum *(sky)*	-a
Gen.	animī	-ōrum	magistrī	-ōrum	puerī	-ōrum	caelī	-ōrum
Dat.	animō	-īs	magistrō	-īs	puerō	-īs	caelō	-īs
Acc.	animum	-ōs	magistrum	-ōs	puerum	-ōs	caelum	-a
Abl.	animō	-īs	magistrō	-īs	puerō	-īs	caelō	-īs

*Adapted from *Graphic Latin Grammar* © Bolchazy-Carducci Publishers, Inc.

THIRD DECLENSION NOUNS

The trademark of the 3rd declension is the ending **-is** in the genitive singular. It is added to the base. All genders are represented in the 3rd declension.[1]

	Masc. Sing.	Masc. Plur.	Fem. Sing.	Fem. Plur.	Neut. Sing.	Neut. Plur.	Masc./Fem. Sing.	Masc./Fem. Plur.
Nom.	mīles (soldier)	mīlitēs	lux (light)	lūcēs	genus (type)	genera	cīvis (citizen)	-ēs
Gen.	mīlitis	-um	lūcis	-um	generis	-um	cīvis	-ium
Dat.	mīlitī	-ibus	lūcī	-ibus	generī	-ibus	cīvī	-ibus
Acc.	mīlitem	-ēs	lūcem	-ēs	genus	-a	cīvem	-ēs (-īs)
Abl.	mīlite	-ibus	lūce	-ibus	genere	-ibus	cīve	-ibus

	Fem. Sing	Fem. Plur.	Neut. Sing.	Neut. Plur.
Nom.	nox (night)	noctēs	mare (sea)	-ia
Gen.	noctis	-ium	maris	-ium
Dat.	noctī	-ibus	marī	-ibus
Acc.	noctem	-ēs (-īs)	mare	-ia
Abl.	nocte	-ibus	marī	-ibus

[1]Nouns ending in **-is** or **-es** that have the same number of syllables in the genitive and the nominative take **-ium** in the genitive plural and, sometimes, **-īs** in the accusative plural.

Nouns whose bases end in double consonants take **-ium** in the genitive plural and, sometimes, **-īs** in the accusative plural.

Neuter nouns ending in **-e, -al,** or **-ar** take **-ī** in the ablative singular, **-ia** in the nominative and accusative plural, and **-ium** in the genitive plural.

FOURTH DECLENSION NOUNS

Most 4th declension nouns are masculine and are formed from the 4th principal part of the verb.

	Masc. Sing.	Masc. Plur.	Fem. Sing.	Fem. Plur.	Neut. Sing.	Neut. Plur.
Nom.	adventus (arrival)	-ūs	domus (house)	-ūs	cornū (horn)	-ua
Gen.	adventūs	-uum	domūs (-ī)	-uum (-ōrum)	cornūs	-uum
Dat.	adventuī (-ū)	-ibus	domuī (-ō)	-ibus	cornū	-ibus
Acc.	adventum	-ūs	domum	-ōs (-ūs)	cornū	-ua
Abl.	adventū	-ibus	domū (-ō)	-ibus	cornū	-ibus

FIFTH DECLENSION NOUNS

Very few nouns in the 5th declension are declined throughout. Most fifth declension nouns are rarely found in the genitive, dative, and ablative plural.

All fifth declension nouns are feminine except **merīdiēs,** which is masculine, and **diēs,** which is either masculine or feminine in the singular but always masculine in the plural.

	Masc./Fem. Sing.	Masc./Fem. Plur.	Fem. Sing.	Fem. Plur.
Nom.	diēs (day)	diēs	rēs (matter)	rēs
Gen.	diēī (diē)	-ērum	reī	rērum
Dat.	diēī (diē)	-ēbus	reī	rēbus
Acc.	diem	-ēs	rem	rēs
Abl.	diē	-ēbus	rē	rēbus

Section 2: Syntax of Cases

NOMINATIVE CASE

1. The subject of a finite verb is nominative. **Aenēās** veniet. *Aeneas will come.*
2. Predicate Nominative (Subject Complement). After the verb *to be* or any form thereof the subject complement replaces an object of the verb. It is in the same case as the subject. Aenēās **vir** Teucrus erat. *Aeneas was a Trojan man.*

GENITIVE CASE

1. Possession. **Phoebī** soror. *Phoebus' sister.* BUT: Rēgīna **mea.** *My queen.* (Possessive adjective)
2. Description/Quality (When a noun is modified). Vir magnae virtūtis . . . *A man of great courage.*
3. Subjective. Adventus Caesaris . . . *The arrival of Caesar.* (If the noun "arrival" were changed to a verb, *Caesar* would become its subject.)
4. Objective. Amor pecūniae . . . *The love of money.* (If the noun "love" were changed to a verb, *money* would be the object of it.) *Note:* These are nouns of action, agency, and feeling.
5. Partitive: **iuvenum** pars. *Part of the young men. Note:* See page 4 and **Reading Help,** line 7, for more information on the "Partitive/ Gen. of the Whole" usage. Cardinal numerals and quīdam take ex or dē plus the ablative case rather than the partitive genitive. The following adjectives modify their noun directly and are not followed by the genitive:

omnis — *each of*	summus — *top of*
tōtus — *whole of*	medius — *middle of*

6. A possessive, partitive, or genitive of quality may stand in the predicate of a sentence. Hic gladius est Caesaris. *This sword is Caesar's.*
7. Preceding causā and gratiā (*for the sake of*) a gerund in the genitive or a noun modified by a gerundive, both genitive, is often used to express purpose. Pugnāndī causā, *for the sake of fighting;* urbis expugnandae causa, *in order to capture the city.*
8. Genitive of indefinite value is expressed by tantī (*of such great value*), quantī (*of how great value*), magnī (*of great value*), parvī (*of little value*), and their comparative or superlative genitive forms. Est mihi tantī. *It is worthwhile (it is of such value) to me.*

DATIVE CASE

1. Indirect object: Fīliō fābulam nārrāvit. *He told his son a story.*
2. Indirect object with an intransitive verb. Crēdite mihi. *Believe me.* Tibi persuādēbō ut discēdās. *I shall persuade you to go away. Note:* When these verbs are in the passive, the indirect object is retained, and the verbs become impersonal. Tibi persuādēbitur ut discēdās. *You will be persuaded to leave.*
3. Indirect Object with Compounds. Some verbs compounded with ad, ante, con, in, ob, post, prae, prō, sub, super in such a way as to change their meanings call for a dative object. Caesar Brūtum exercituī praefēcit. *Caesar put Brutus in charge of the army.*
4. Dative of Possession (with the verb *to be*). Imperātōrī est gladius. *The commander has a sword.*
5. Dative of agent is used with the gerundive and some of the perfect passive constructions to show the "doer" of the action. Oppidum Caesarī est oppugnandum. *The town ought to be besieged by Caesar.* Mihi dēlīberātum est. *I have deliberated.*
6. Dative of Purpose. Vēnit auxiliō castrīs. *He came as an aid to the camp.* The following words are most commonly used with this construction: auxilium - *aid*, praesidium - *guard*, cūra - *care*, subsidium - *reserve*
7. Dative of Reference. The person or thing affected in the sentence. . . . quibus locus parātur . . . *for whom a place is being made ready. Note:* When the datives of purpose and reference are used together, they are called the double dative. Flūmen erat magnō impedīmentō Gallīs. *The river was a great hindrance to the Gauls.*
8. Dative of Separation. Occasionally, after compounds with ab, dē, ex, ad, the dative occurs instead of the usual ablative. Hunc timōrem mihi ēripe. *Take this fear from me.*
9. The dative occurs with adjectives of *fitness* (aptus), *nearness* (proximus), *likeness* (similis), *friendliness* (amīcus), and their opposites. Gallī sunt proximī Germānīs. *The Gauls are nearest the Germans.*

ACCUSATIVE CASE

1. Direct Object of a transitive verb. Brūtus Caesarem vulneravit. *Brutus wounded Caesar.*
2. Subject of the infinitive: In indirect statements and after iubeō (*order*), patior (*allow*), and sinō (*permit*), the subject of the infinitive goes into the accusative case. Dīxit ducem fūgisse. *He said that the leader had fled.*
3. Predicate accusative or object complement where a second accusative is used after verbs like appellō (*name*), dēligō (*choose*), faciō (*make*), creō (*elect*). Pompeium cōnsulem creāvērunt. *They elected Pompey consul.*
4. After verbs of asking and teaching, two accusatives are found: one of the direct object, the other the things asked or taught. Mē sententiam rogāvit. *He asked me my opinion.*
5. Duration of Time (How Long). Multās hōrās pugnāvērunt. *They fought for many hours.*
6. Extent of Space. Multa mīlia passuum iter fēcērunt. *They marched many miles.*
7. Object of certain prepositions: These prepositions take an accusative object: ad, ante, circum, contrā, inter, intrā, ob, per, post, prope, propter, sub, super, trāns, ultrā. Per hōs annōs . . . *During these years . . .*
8. Ad with the accusative gerund or a noun modified by the gerundive, both accusative, is often used to express purpose. ad pugnandum, *for the purpose of fighting;* ad urbem expugnandam, *in order to capture the city.*

ABLATIVE CASE

1.   Object of certain prepositions (all those not listed as governing the accusative case). The more common ones are ā/ab, cum, dē, ē/ex, in, prae, prō, sine, sub.

2.   Personal agent, expressed with a passive verb and a person, with ā /ab. Caesar ā Brūtō interfectus est. *Caesar was killed by Brutus.*

3.   Separation. With a verb of motion, the ablative is always used. Hostēs ā fīnibus prohibent. *They keep the enemy from their territory.*

4.   Place from which. Ex urbe ēgressus est. *He left the city.*

5.   Ablative of Cause. Timōre commōtus est. *He was frightened (moved by fear).*

6.   Ablative (of Means) with "<u>PUFFV</u> deponent verbs": <u>P</u>otior (*gain*), <u>Ū</u>tor (*use*), <u>F</u>ruor (*enjoy*), <u>F</u>ungor (*perform*), <u>V</u>escor (*feed on*). With these, the ablative is generally used. Gladiīs ūsus est. *He used swords.*

7.   Respect/Specification. This ablative tells in what respect something is done or is true. Mōns magnus altitūdine . . . *A mountain great in height . . .*

8.   Degree of Difference. After comparatives, this ablative shows the extent or degree to which the objects differ. Puer est altior quam puella ūnō pede. *The boy is taller than the girl by a foot.*

9.   Ablative of manner, telling "how," may omit the usual cum if the noun is modified. Magnā (cum) celeritāte fūgērunt. *They fled with great speed.*

10.   Accompaniment (regularly with cum). Cum coniugibus . . . *With wives . . .*

11.   Ablative of means or instrument of an action occurs without a preposition in most cases. Mīlitēs gladiīs vulnerātī erant. *The soldiers had been wounded by swords.*

12.   Ablative of time when, without a preposition. Prīmō annō . . . *In the first year . . .*

13.   Ablative Absolute. See Major Review #2.

14.   Description/Quality. Vir magnā virtūte . . . *A man of great courage.*

VOCATIVE CASE

The vocative case is used for direct address. See Rapid Review #2.

LOCATIVE CASE

The locative case is used only to indicate "place where" or "place at which" with names of towns or cities, humus (*soil*), domus (*home*), and rūs (*the country*). In all other cases the ablative of "place where" with the preposition *in* is used. The locative endings are:

	Sing.	*Plur.*
1st Declension	**-ae**	**-īs**
2nd Declension	**-ī**	**-īs**
3rd Declension	**-ī or -e**	**-ibus**

Rōmae — *in Rome,* **domī** — *at home,* **rūrī** — *in the country*

Section 3: Pronouns

PERSONAL PRONOUNS

		1st Person					2nd Person		
	Sing.		*Plur.*			*Sing.*		*Plur.*	
Nom.	ego	*I*	nōs	*we*	tū	*you*	vōs	*you*
Gen.	meī	*of me*	nostrum, nostrī	*of us*	tuī	*of you*	vestrum, vestrī	*of you*
Dat.	mihi	*to me*	nōbīs	*to us*	tibi	*to you*	vōbīs	*to you*
Acc.	mē	*me*	nōs	*us*	tē	*you*	vōs	*you*
Abl.	mē	*by, etc., me*	nōbīs	*by, etc., us*	tē	*by, etc., you*	vōbīs	*by, etc., you*

3rd Person: A demonstrative, usually **is, ea, id,** serves as a substitute for the missing personal pronoun of the 3rd person.

INTERROGATIVE PRONOUNS

See Rapid Review #6. The interrogative pronoun, as its name implies, introduces a question. **Quis** means *who,* and **quid** means *what.* Declension is like the relative, **quis** for **quī, quid** for **quod,** with the plural declined the same.

THE INTENSIVE PRONOUN IPSE

Ipse is used to emphasize nouns and pronouns of any person and may agree with the pronoun subject contained in the verb. Lēgātus ipse haec dīxit. *The envoy himself said these things.* Ipse haec dīxit. *He himself said these things.*

Sing.			*Plur.*		
ipse	ipsa	ipsum	ipsī	ipsae	ipsa
ipsīus	ipsīus	ipsīus	ipsōrum	ipsārum	ipsōrum
ipsī	ipsī	ipsī	ipsīs	ipsīs	ipsīs
ipsum	ipsam	ipsum	ipsōs	ipsās	ipsa
ipsō	ipsā	ipsō	ipsīs	ipsīs	ipsīs

RELATIVE PRONOUNS

Quī, quae, quod *(who, which)* is the most commonly used of the relative pronouns (or adjectives).

Sing.			*Plur.*		
Masc.	*Fem.*	*Neut.*	*Masc.*	*Fem.*	*Neut.*
quī	quae	quod	quī	quae	quae
cuius	cuius	cuius	quōrum	quārum	quōrum
cui	cui	cui	quibus	quibus	quibus
quem	quam	quod	quōs	quās	quae
quō	quā	quō	quibus	quibus	quibus

Section 4: Adjectives and Adverbs

FIRST AND SECOND DECLENSION ADJECTIVES

Adjectives agree with their nouns in case, number, and gender. Those in the predicate after **sum** *(be)* agree with the subject, as in English. Most masculine adjectives are declined like **ager, puer,** or **dominus;** neuter adjectives like **caelum;** and feminine adjectives like **terra.**

	Masculine		Feminine		Neuter	
	Sing.	*Plur.*	*Sing.*	*Plur.*	*Sing.*	*Plur.*
Nom.	bonus	-ī	bona	-ae	bonum	-a
Gen.	bonī	-ōrum	bonae	-ārum	bonī	-ōrum
Dat.	bonō	-īs	bonae	-īs	bonō	-īs
Acc.	bonum	-ōs	bonam	-ās	bonum	-a
Abl.	bonō	-īs	bonā	-īs	bonō	-īs

THIRD DECLENSION ADJECTIVES

Third declension adjectives fall into three distinct categories: (1) *three-termination,* with separate endings for all three genders, like **ācer;** (2) *two-termination,* with the same endings for masculine and feminine, like **omnis;** (3) *one-termination,* with the nominative singular the same in all genders, like **potēns.** The *comparative* of all adjectives, like **longior** (4), is declined like a 3rd declension <u>noun</u> (-e in abl. sing., -um in gen. plur., and -a in neuter nom. and accus. plurals). The forms of **plūs** (5) are unique. Present participles are declined like **potēns.**

(1) ācer *(keen)*

	Masc.		Fem.		Neut.	
	Sing.	*Plur.*	*Sing.*	*Plur.*	*Sing.*	*Plur.*
Nom.	ācer	ācrēs	ācris	ācrēs	ācre	ācria
Gen.	ācris	-ium	ācris	-ium	ācris	-ium
Dat.	ācrī	-ibus	ācrī	-ibus	ācrī	-ibus
Acc.	ācrem	-ēs (-īs)	ācrem	-ēs (-īs)	ācre	-ia
Abl.	ācrī	-ibus	ācrī	-ibus	ācrī	-ibus

(2) omnis *(each, every; plur. all)*

	Masc. & Fem.		Neut.	
	Sing.	*Plur.*	*Sing.*	*Plur.*
Nom.	omnis	-ēs	omne	-ia
Gen.	omnis	-ium	omnis	-ium
Dat.	omnī	-ibus	omnī	-ibus
Acc.	omnem	-ēs (-īs)	omne	-ia
Abl.	omnī	-ibus	omnī	-ibus

(3) potēns *(powerful)*

	Masc. & Fem.		Neut.	
	Sing.	*Plur.*	*Sing.*	*Plur.*
Nom.	potēns	potentēs	potēns	potentia
Gen.	potentis	-ium	potentis	-ium
Dat.	potentī	-ibus	potentī	-ibus
Acc.	potentem	-ēs (-īs)	potēns	-ia
Abl.	potentī (-e)	-ibus	potentī (-e)	-ibus

(4) longior *(longer)*

	Masc. & Fem.		Neut.	
	Sing.	*Plur.*	*Sing.*	*Plur.*
Nom.	longior	longiōrēs	longius	longiōra
Gen.	longiōris	-um	longiōris	-um
Dat.	longiōrī	-ibus	longiōrī	-ibus
Acc.	longiōrem	-ēs (-īs)	longius	-a
Abl.	longiōre	-ibus	longiōre	-ibus

(5) plūs *(more)*

	Masc. & Fem.	Neut.	
	Plur.	*Sing.*	*Plur.*
Nom.	plūrēs	plūs	plūra
Gen.	-ium	plūris	-ium
Dat.	-ibus	plūrī	-ibus
Acc.	-ēs (-īs)	plūs	-a
Abl.	-ibus	plūre	-ibus

THE IRREGULAR ADJECTIVES

There are ten adjectives (<u>ŪNUS</u> + the <u>ŪNUS NAUTA</u> [or "naughty nine"] adjectives) which are irregular in the genitive and dative singulars. The plurals of these words are declined like **bonus, -a, -um.**

Ūnus, -a, -um	*one, alone*	Neuter, tra, -trum	*neither*
Ūllus, -a, -um	*any*	Alius, alia, aliud	*(an)other*
Nūllus, -a, -um	*not any, no, none*	Ūterque, ūtraque, ūtrumque	*each (of 2)*
Ūter, ūtra, ūtrum	*which (of 2)?*	Tōtus, -a, -um	*whole, all*
Sōlus, -a, -um	*alone, only*	Alter, -era, -erum	*the other*

tōtus *(whole, all)*

	Masc.	Fem.	Neut.
Nom.	tōtus	tōta	tōtum
Gen.	tōtīus	tōtīus	tōtīus
Dat.	tōtī	tōtī	tōtī
Acc.	tōtum	tōtam	tōtum
Abl.	tōtō	tōtā	tōtō

Comparison of Adjectives

See Rapid Review #8 for more on the comparison of adjectives. There are three degrees of comparison in Latin, just as there are in English: *positive, comparative,* and *superlative*. The *comparative* is formed by adding **-ior** for the masculine and feminine, and **-ius** for the neuter to the base of the *positive*. The *superlative* is usually formed by adding **-issimus, -a, -um** to the base. The *positive* is declined like **bonus** for 1st and 2nd declension, like **omnis** for 3rd declension adjectives. The *comparative* is declined like **longior** above. The *superlative* is declined like **bonus.**

Note: Six adjectives ending in **-lis** (facilis, difficilis, similis, dissimilis, gracilis, humilis) add **-limus** instead of **-issimus** to the base to form the *superlative:* (facilis, facilior, facillimus)

Note: Adjectives ending in **-er** add **-rimus** instead of **-issimus** to form the *superlative*.

miser, -a, -um	miserior, miserius	miserrimus, -a, -um
ācer, ācris, ācre	ācrior, ācrius	ācerrimus, -a, -um

Note: Adjectives ending in **-ius** or **-eus** add **magis** to form the comparative and **maximē** to form the superlative: idōneus, magis idōneus, maximē idōneus.

Regular Forms

Positive	Comparative	Superlative
longus, -a, -um	long**ior**, long**ius**	long**issimus, -a, -um**
fortis, forte	fort**ior**, fort**ius**	fort**issimus, -a, -um**

Irregular Comparisons

Positive	Comparative	Superlative
bonus *(good)*	melior	optimus
malus *(bad)*	peior	pessimus
magnus *(large)*	maior	maximus
multus *(much)*	plūs	plūrimus
multī *(many)*	plūrēs	plūrimī
parvus *(small)*	minor	minimus

Section 5: Verbs, Indicative and Imperative

REGULAR VERBS

In Latin the verb is especially important. It causes the subject either to act or to be acted upon. It expresses person, number, tense, voice, and mood. It includes four possible participles, five common infinitives, the gerund, and the supine.

The present, imperfect, and the future indicative tenses, active and passive, are formed from the *present stem*, obtained by removing the -re from the present infinitive. The three perfect indicative active tenses are formed from the *perfect stem*, obtained by removing the -ī from the third principal part. The three perfect indicative passive tenses are formed from the fourth principal part, the entire *perfect passive participle*.

FIRST CONJUGATION

PRINCIPAL PARTS OF PARŌ

parō	1st Sing. Pres. Act. Ind.	*I prepare*
parāre	Pres. Act. Inf.	*to prepare*
parāvī	1st Sing. Perf. Act. Ind.	*I prepared, I (have) prepared*
parātum	Perf. Pass. Part.	*(having been) prepared*

INDICATIVE ACTIVE

Present
parō *I prepare*
parās *you prepare*
parat *he prepares*
parāmus *we prepare*
parātis *you prepare*
parant *they prepare*

Perfect
parāvī *I (have) prepared*
parāvistī *you (have) prepared*
parāvit *he (has) prepared*
parāvimus *we (have) prepared*
parāvistis *you (have) prepared*
parāvērunt *they (have) prepared*

Imperfect
parābam *I was preparing*
parābās *you were preparing*
parābat *he was preparing*
parābāmus *we were preparing*
parābātis *you were preparing*
parābant *they were preparing*

Pluperfect
parāveram *I had prepared*
parāverās *you had prepared*
parāverat *he had prepared*
parāverāmus *we had prepared*
parāverātis *you had prepared*
parāverant *they had prepared*

Future
parābō *I shall prepare*
parābis *you will prepare*
parābit *he will prepare*
parābimus *we will prepare*
parābitis *you will prepare*
parābunt *they will prepare*

Future Perfect
parāverō *I shall have prepared*
parāveris *you will have prepared*
parāverit *he will have prepared*
parāverimus *we will have prepared*
parāveritis *you will have prepared*
parāverint *they will have prepared*

INDICATIVE PASSIVE

Present
paror *I am (being) prepared*
parāris *you are prepared*
parātur *he is prepared*
parāmur *we are prepared*
parāminī *you are prepared*
parantur *they are prepared*

Perfect
parātus, -a, -um **sum** *I was (have been) prepared*
parātus, -a, -um **es** *you were (have been) prepared*
parātus, -a, -um **est** *he was (has been) prepared*
parātī, -ae, -a **sumus** *we were (have been) prepared*
parātī, -ae, -a **estis** *you were (have been) prepared*
parātī, -ae, -a **sunt** *they were (have been) prepared*

Imperfect
parābar *I was being prepared*
parābāris *you were prepared*
parābātur *he was prepared*
parābāmur *we were prepared*
parābāminī *you were prepared*
parābantur *they were prepared*

Pluperfect
parātus, -a, -um **eram** *I had been prepared*
parātus, -a, -um **erās** *you had been prepared*
parātus, -a, -um **erat** *he had been prepared*
parātī, -ae, -a **erāmus** *we had been prepared*
parātī, -ae, -a **erātis** *you had been prepared*
parātī, -ae, -a **erant** *they had been prepared*

Future
parābor *I shall be prepared*
parāberis* *you will be prepared*
parābitur *he will be prepared*
parābimur *we shall be prepared*
parābiminī *you will be prepared*
parābuntur *they will be prepared*

Future Perfect
parātus, -a, -um **erō** *I shall have been prepared*
parātus, -a, -um **eris** *you will have been prepared*
parātus, -a, -um **erit** *he will have been prepared*
parātī, -ae, -a **erimus** *we shall have been prepared*
parātī, -ae, -a **eritis** *you will have been prepared*
parātī, -ae, -a **erunt** *they will have been prepared*

*The expected **-biris** changes to **-beris** for pronunciation reasons.

IMPERATIVE ACTIVE

PRESENT
Sing.: parā   *prepare*
Plur.: parāte   *prepare*

SECOND CONJUGATION

PRINCIPAL PARTS OF HABEŌ

habeō *I have*   **habēre** *to have*   **habuī** *I (have) had*   **habitum** *(having been) held*

INDICATIVE ACTIVE

Present	Perfect
habeō	habuī
habēs	habuistī
habet	habuit
habēmus	habuimus
habētis	habuistis
habent	habuērunt

Imperfect	Pluperfect
habēbam	habueram
habēbās	habuerās
habēbat	habuerat
habēbāmus	habuerāmus
habēbātis	habuerātis
habēbant	habuerant

Future	Future Perfect
habēbō	habuerō
habēbis	habueris
habēbit	habuerit
habēbimus	habuerimus
habēbitis	habueritis
habēbunt	habuerint

INDICATIVE PASSIVE

Present	Perfect
habeor	habitus, -a, -um **sum**
habēris	habitus, -a, -um **es**
habētur	habitus, -a, -um **est**
habēmur	habitī, -ae, -a **sumus**
habēminī	habitī, -ae, -a **estis**
habentur	habitī, -ae, -a **sunt**

Imperfect	Pluperfect
habēbar	habitus, -a, -um **eram**
habēbāris	habitus, -a, -um **erās**
habēbātur	habitus, -a, -um **erat**
habēbāmur	habitī, -ae, -a **erāmus**
habēbāminī	habitī, -ae, -a **erātis**
habēbantur	habitī, -ae, -a **erant**

Future	Future Perfect
habēbor	habitus, -a, -um **erō**
habēberis*	habitus, -a, -um **eris**
habēbitur	habitus, -a, -um **erit**
habēbimur	habitī, -ae, -a **erimus**
habēbiminī	habitī, -ae, -a **eritis**
habēbuntur	habitī, -ae, -a **erunt**

*The expected **-biris** changes to **-beris** for pronunciation reasons.

IMPERATIVE ACTIVE

PRESENT

Sing.: habē
Plur.: habēte

THIRD CONJUGATION

PRINCIPAL PARTS OF DŪCŌ
dūcō *I lead*   **dūcere** *to lead*   **dūxī** *I (have) led*   **ductum** *(having been) led*

The future active of the third conjugation is formed by adding -am, -ēs, -et, etc. to the present stem minus **-e.** To form the passive, -ar, -ēris, -ētur, etc. are added to the present stem minus **-e.**

INDICATIVE ACTIVE

Present	Perfect
dūcō	dūxī
dūcis	dūxistī
dūcit	dūxit
dūcimus	dūximus
dūcitis	dūxistis
dūcunt	dūxērunt

Imperfect	Pluperfect
dūcēbam	dūxeram
dūcēbās	dūxerās
dūcēbat	dūxerat
dūcēbāmus	dūxerāmus
dūcēbātis	dūxerātis
dūcēbant	dūxerant

Future	Future Perfect
dūcam	dūxerō
dūcēs	dūxeris
dūcet	dūxerit
dūcēmus	dūxerimus
dūcētis	dūxeritis
dūcent	dūxerint

INDICATIVE PASSIVE

Present	Perfect
dūcor	ductus, -a, -um **sum**
dūceris*	ductus, -a, -um **es**
dūcitur	ductus, -a, -um **est**
dūcimur	ductī, -ae, -a **sumus**
dūciminī	ductī, -ae, -a **estis**
dūcuntur	ductī, -ae, -a **sunt**

Imperfect	Pluperfect
dūcēbar	ductus, -a, -um **eram**
dūcēbāris	ductus, -a, -um **erās**
dūcēbātur	ductus, -a, -um **erat**
dūcēbāmur	ductī, -ae, -a **erāmus**
dūcēbāminī	ductī, -ae, -a **erātis**
dūcēbantur	ductī, -ae, -a **erant**

Future	Future Perfect
dūcar	ductus, -a, -um **erō**
dūcēris	ductus, -a, -um **eris**
dūcētur	ductus, -a, -um **erit**
dūcēmur	ductī, -ae, -a **erimus**
dūcēminī	ductī, -ae, -a **eritis**
dūcentur	ductī, -ae, -a **erunt**

*The expected **-iris** changes to **-eris** for pronunciation reasons.

IMPERATIVE ACTIVE
Sing.: dūc[1]
Plur.: dūcite

[1]There are four verbs whose imperative omits the final "e" in the singular: dīc, dūc, fac, fer.

THE -IO VERBS OF THE 3RD CONJUGATION

PRINCIPAL PARTS OF CAPIŌ
capiō   *I seize*
capere *to seize*
cēpī   *I (have) seized*
captum *(having been) seized*

INDICATIVE
The six tenses of the indicative active are conjugated like audiō (4th conjugation) except that the -i of capiō is short throughout the present tense.

In the indicative passive, the second person singular, present passive, differs from its parallel in audiō: caperis, audīris.

IMPERATIVE ACTIVE
Sing.: cape
Plur.: capite

Fourth Conjugation

PRINCIPAL PARTS OF AUDIŌ

audiō	*I hear*
audīre	*to hear*
audīvī	*I (have) heard*
audītum	*(having been) heard*

INDICATIVE ACTIVE

Present	*Perfect*
audiō	audīvī
audīs	audīvistī
audit	audīvit
audīmus	audīvimus
audītis	audīvistis
audiunt	audīvērunt

Imperfect	*Pluperfect*
audiēbam	audīveram
audiēbās	audīverās
audiēbat	audīverat
audiēbāmus	audīverāmus
audiēbātis	audīverātis
audiēbant	audīverant

Future	*Future Perfect*
audiam	audīverō
audiēs	audīveris
audiet	audīverit
audiēmus	audīverimus
audiētis	audīveritis
audient	audīverint

INDICATIVE PASSIVE

Present	*Perfect*
audior	audītus, -a, -um **sum**
audīris	audītus, -a, -um **es**
audītur	audītus, -a, -um **est**
audīmur	audītī, -ae, -a **sumus**
audīminī	audītī, -ae, -a **estis**
audiuntur	audītī, -ae, -a **sunt**

Imperfect	*Pluperfect*
audiēbar	audītus, -a, -um **eram**
audiēbāris	audītus, -a, -um **erās**
audiēbātur	audītus, -a, -um **erat**
audiēbāmur	audītī, -ae, -a **erāmus**
audiēbāminī	audītī, -ae, -a **erātis**
audiēbantur	audītī, -ae, -a **erant**

Future	*Future Perfect*
audiar	audītus, -a, -um **erō**
audiēris	audītus, -a, -um **eris**
audiētur	audītus, -a, -um **erit**
audiēmur	audītī, -ae, -a **erimus**
audiēminī	audītī, -ae, -a **eritis**
audientur	audītī, -ae, -a **erunt**

IMPERATIVE ACTIVE

Sing.: audī
Plur.: audīte

Deponent Verbs (passive in form; active in meaning)

See Rapid Review #10 for a more complete treatment of deponent verbs. There are deponent verbs in all four conjugations. All are regularly passive in form. Exceptions are the future infinitive and the present and future participles, which are active in form.

The Irregular Verb Sum

See Rapid Review #11 for more on the irregular verbs.

PRINCIPAL PARTS

sum *I am*   **esse** *to be*   **fuī** *I was (have been)*   **futūrus** *being about to be*

INDICATIVE

Present	*Imperfect*	*Future*	*Perfect*	*Pluperfect*	*Future Perfect*
sum	eram	erō	fuī	fueram	fuerō
es	erās	eris	fuistī	fuerās	fueris
est	erat	erit	fuit	fuerat	fuerit
sumus	erāmus	erimus	fuimus	fuerāmus	fuerimus
estis	erātis	eritis	fuistis	fuerātis	fueritis
sunt	erant	erunt	fuērunt	fuerant	fuerint

THE IRREGULAR VERB POSSUM

PRINCIPAL PARTS

possum *I am able*   **posse** *to be able*   **potuī** *I was (have been) able*

INDICATIVE

Present	*Imperfect*	*Future*	*Perfect*	*Pluperfect*	*Future Perfect*
possum	poteram	poterō	potuī	potueram	potuerō
potes	poterās	poteris	potuistī	potuerās	potueris
potest	poterat	poterit	potuit	potuerat	potuerit
possumus	poterāmus	poterimus	potuimus	potuerāmus	potuerimus
potestis	poterātis	poteritis	potuistis	potuerātis	potueritis
possunt	poterant	poterunt	potuērunt	potuerant	potuerint

THE IRREGULAR VERB FERŌ

PRINCIPAL PARTS

ferō *I bear*   **ferre** *to bear*   **tulī** *I bore, have borne*   **lātum** *(having been) borne*

INDICATIVE ACTIVE

Present	*Imperfect*	*Future*	*Perfect*	*Pluperfect*	*Future Perfect*
ferō	ferēbam	feram	tulī	tuleram	tulerō
fers	ferēbās	ferēs	tulistī	tulerās	tuleris
fert	ferēbat	feret	tulit	tulerat	tulerit
ferimus	etc.	etc.	tulimus	etc.	etc.
fertis			tulistis		
ferunt			tulērunt		

INDICATIVE PASSIVE

Present	*Imperfect*	*Future*	*Perfect*	*Pluperfect*	*Future Perfect*
feror	ferēbar	ferar	lātus, -a, -um **sum**	lātus, -a, -um **eram**	lātus, -a, -um **erō**
ferris	ferēbāris	ferēris	lātus, -a, -um **es**	lātus, -a, -um **erās**	lātus, -a, -um **eris**
fertur	ferēbātur	ferētur	lātus, -a, -um **est**	lātus, -a, -um **erat**	lātus, -a, -um **erit**
ferimur	etc.	etc.	etc.	etc.	etc.
feriminī					
feruntur					

IMPERATIVE ACTIVE

Sing.: fer
Plur.: ferte

THE IRREGULAR VERB EŌ[1]

PRINCIPAL PARTS

eō *I go*   **īre** *to go*   **iī (īvī)** *I went, have gone*   **itum (est)** *it has been gone*

INDICATIVE

Present	*Imperfect*	*Future*	*Perfect*	*Pluperfect*	*Future Perfect*
eō	ībam	ībō	iī	ieram	ierō
īs	ībās	ībis	iistī	ierās	ieris
it	ībat	ībit	iit	ierat	ierit
īmus	ībāmus	ībimus	iimus	ierāmus	ierimus
ītis	ībātis	ībitis	iistis	ierātis	ieritis
eunt	ībant	ībunt	iērunt	ierant	ierint

IMPERATIVE

Present
Sing.: ī
Plur.: īte

[1]Adeō, ineō, and transeō are transitive and may therefore be conjugated in the passive. Queō and nequeō are conjugated like eō.

The Irregular Verbs Volō, Nōlō, and Mālō

Nōlō is curtailed from nō(n vo)lō or n(ē-v)olō, while mālō is curtailed from ma(gis-vo)lō.

   Note: With the exception of the present tense, the forms of nōlō and mālō are similar to volō. For forms not given below, see volō, which is complete. Mālō and volō do not have imperative forms. Mālō is also deficient in participles.

PRINCIPAL PARTS
volō *I wish, am willing*   **velle** *to wish, be willing*   **voluī** *I (have) wished, was willing*

INDICATIVE

Present	Imperfect	Future	Perfect	Pluperfect	Future Perfect
volō	volēbam	volam	voluī	volueram	voluerō
vīs	volēbās	volēs	voluistī	voluerās	volueris
vult	volēbat	volet	voluit	voluerat	voluerit
volumus	volēbāmus	volēmus	voluimus	voluerāmus	voluerimus
vultis	volēbātis	volētis	voluistis	voluerātis	volueritis
volunt	volēbant	volent	voluērunt	voluerant	voluerint

PRINCIPAL PARTS
mālō *I prefer*   **mālle** *to prefer*   **māluī** *I (have) preferred*

INDICATIVE
Present
mālō
māvīs
māvult
mālumus
māvultis
mālunt

PRINCIPAL PARTS
nōlō *I do not wish*   **nōlle** *to be unwilling*   **nōluī** *I was (have been) unwilling, did not wish*

INDICATIVE
Present
nōlō
nōn vīs
nōn vult
nōlumus
nōn vultis
nōlunt

IMPERATIVE[1]
Sing.: nōlī
Plur.: nōlīte

[1]These forms, plus a complementary infinitive, express a negative command.

The Irregular Verb Fīō

Note: Fīō is the irregular passive of faciō. Even though it is conjugated actively in the present, imperfect, future, it always has passive meaning.

PRINCIPAL PARTS
fīō *I am made*   **fierī** *to be made*   **factus sum** *I was (have been) made*

INDICATIVE

Present	Imperfect	Future	Perfect	Pluperfect	Future Perfect
fīō	fīēbam	fīam	factus, -a, -um **sum**	factus, -a, -um **eram**	factus, -a, -um **erō**
fīs	fīēbās	fīēs	*etc.*	*etc.*	*etc.*
fit	fīēbat	fīet			
fīmus	fīēbāmus	fīēmus			
fītis	fīēbātis	fīētis			
fīunt	fīēbant	fīent			

Section 6: Infinitives

See Major Review #1 for a complete treatment of infinitive formation, translation, and basic usages.

FIRST CONJUGATION

INFINITIVES

ACTIVE			PASSIVE		
Present:	parāre	to prepare	*Present:*	parārī	to be prepared
Perfect:	parāvisse	to have prepared	*Perfect:*	parātus esse	to have been prepared
Future:	parātūrus esse	to be about to prepare			

SECOND CONJUGATION

INFINITIVES

ACTIVE		PASSIVE	
Present:	habēre	*Present:*	habērī
Perfect:	habuisse	*Perfect:*	habitus esse
Future:	habitūrus esse		

THIRD CONJUGATION

INFINITIVES

ACTIVE		PASSIVE	
Pres.:	dūcere	*Pres.:*	dūcī[1]
Perf.:	dūxisse	*Perf.:*	ductus esse
Fut.:	ductūrus esse		

[1]To form the present passive infinitive, replace the -ere of the active form with -ī.

THIRD -IO CONJUGATION

INFINITIVES

ACTIVE		PASSIVE	
Pres.:	capere	*Pres.:*	capī
Perf.:	cēpisse	*Perf.:*	captus esse
Fut.:	captūrus esse		

FOURTH CONJUGATION

INFINITIVES[2]

ACTIVE		PASSIVE	
Pres.:	audīre	*Pres.:*	audīrī
Perf.:	audīvisse	*Perf.:*	audītus esse
Fut.:	audītūrus esse		

[2]The present passive infinitive of the 1st, 2nd, and 4th conjugations is formed by replacing the final -e of the present active infinitive with an -ī.

IRREGULAR VERBS

SUM: INFINITIVES		POSSUM: INFINITIVES		EŌ: INFINITIVES		FERŌ: INFINITIVES—ACTIVE		INFINITIVES—PASSIVE	
Pres.:	esse	*Pres.:*	posse	*Pres.:*	īre	*Pres.:*	ferre	*Pres.:*	ferrī
Perf.:	fuisse	*Perf.:*	potuisse	*Perf.:*	iisse	*Perf.:*	tulisse	*Perf.:*	lātus esse
Fut.:	futūrus esse			*Fut.:*	itūrus esse	*Fut.:*	lātūrus esse		

VOLŌ: INFINITIVES		NŌLŌ: INFINITIVES		MĀLŌ: INFINITIVES		FĪŌ: INFINITIVES	
Pres.:	velle	*Pres.:*	nōlle	*Pres.:*	mālle	*Pres.:*	fierī
Perf.:	voluisse	*Perf.:*	nōluisse	*Perf.:*	māluisse	*Perf.:*	factus esse

DEPONENT VERBS

Pres.:	loquī	to say
Perf.:	locūtus esse	to have said
Fut.:	locūtūrus esse	to be about to say

Section 7: Participles

See Major Review #2 for a complete treatment of participle formation, declension, translation, and basic usages.

FIRST CONJUGATION

PARTICIPLES

Present Active:	parāns	*preparing*
Perfect Passive:	parātus, -a, -um	*(having been) prepared*
Future Active:	parātūrus, -a, -um	*(being) about to prepare*
Fut. Pass. (G'ndive):	parandus, -a, -um	*about (fit) to be prepared*

SECOND CONJUGATION

PARTICIPLES

Present Active:	habēns
Perfect Passive:	habitus, -a, -um
Future Active:	habitūrus, -a, -um
Fut. Pass. (G'ndive):	habendus, -a, -um

THIRD CONJUGATION

PARTICIPLES

Present Active:	dūcēns
Perfect Passive:	ductus, -a, -um
Future Active:	ductūrus, -a, -um
Fut. Pass. (G'ndive):	ducendus, -a, -um

THIRD -IO CONJUGATION

PARTICIPLES

Present Active:	capiēns
Perfect Passive:	captus, -a, -um
Future Active:	captūrus, -a, -um
Fut. Pass. (G'ndive):	capiendus, -a, -um

FOURTH CONJUGATION

PARTICIPLES

Present Active:	audiēns
Perfect Passive:	audītus, -a, -um
Future Active:	audītūrus, -a, -um
Fut. Pass. (G'ndive):	audiendus, -a, -um

IRREGULAR VERBS

SUM:
PARTICIPLES
Fut. Act.: futūrus, -a, -um

POSSUM:
PARTICIPLES
Pres. Act.: potēns

EŌ:
PARTICIPLES
Pres. Act.: iēns (euntis)
Fut. Act: itūrus, -a, -um
Fut. Pass. (G'ndive): eundus, -a, -um

FERŌ:
PARTICIPLES
Pres. Act.: ferēns
Fut. Act.: lātūrus, -a, -um
Perf. Pass: lātus, -a, -um
Fut. Pass. (G'ndive): ferendus, -a, -um

VOLŌ:
PARTICIPLES
Pres. Act.: volēns

NŌLŌ:
PARTICIPLES
Pres. Act.: nōlēns

FĪŌ:
PARTICIPLES
Pres. Act.: (none)
Perf. Pass.: factus, -a, -um
Fut. Pass. (G'ndive): faciendus, -a, -um

DEPONENT VERBS

Pres.:	loquēns (3rd conjug.)
Perf.:	locūtus, -a, -um
Fut.:	locūtūrus, -a, -um
Fut. Pass. (G'ndive):	loquendus, -a, -um

Section 8: Gerunds

FIRST CONJUGATION

GERUND
(Nom.:	parāre	*preparing)*
Gen.:	parandī	*of preparing*
Dat.:	parandō	*for preparing*
Acc.:	parandum	*preparing*
Abl.:	parandō	*by preparing*

SECOND CONJUGATION

GERUND
(Nom.:	habēre)
Gen.:	habendī
Dat.:	habendō
Acc.:	habendum
Abl.:	habendō

THIRD CONJUGATION

GERUND
(Nom.:	dūcere)
Gen.:	dūcendī
Dat.:	dūcendō
Acc.:	dūcendum
Abl.:	dūcendō

THIRD -IO CONJUGATION

GERUND
(Nom.:	capere)
Gen.:	capiendī
Dat.:	capiendō
Acc.:	capiendum
Abl.:	capiendō

FOURTH CONJUGATION

GERUND
(Nom.:	audīre)
Gen.:	audiendī
Dat.:	audiendō
Acc.:	audiendum
Abl.:	audiendō

IRREGULAR VERBS

Note: Only **eō** and **ferō** of the irregular verbs have gerunds.

Eō
GERUND
(Nom.:	īre)
Gen.:	eundī
Dat.:	eundō
Acc.:	eundum
Abl.:	eundō

Ferō
GERUND
(Nom.:	ferre)
Gen.:	ferendī
Dat.:	ferendō
Acc.:	ferendum
Abl.:	ferendō

DEPONENT VERBS

Loquor
GERUND
(Nom.:	loquī)
Gen.:	loquendī
Dat.:	loquendō
Acc.:	loquendum
Abl.:	loquendō

BIBLIOGRAPHY

While by no means intended to be a complete bibliography (scholarly work on these three poets and their poetry is vast), we did want to alert teachers and students to those works we have consulted most frequently, both for our own day-to-day teaching and in the preparation of this book. Additional stimulating ideas abound in them. All informal citations in the text refer to items listed here.

CATULLUS

J. Ferguson, *Catullus*. Lawrence, KS, 1985.

P. Y. Forsyth, *Catullus. A Teaching Text*. Lanham, MD, 1986.

D. H. Garrison, *The Student's Catullus*. Norman, OK, 1995.

R. O. A. M. Lyne, *Selections from Catullus: Handbook*. Cambridge, 1975.

K. Quinn, *Catullus. The Poems*. London, 1973.

S. G. P. Small, *Catullus. A Reader's Guide to the Poems*. Lanham, MD, 1983.

HORACE

R. Ancona, *Horace. Selected* Odes *and* Satire I. 9. Wauconda, 1999.

H. V. Bender, *A Horace Reader for Advanced Placement*. Newburyport, MA, 1998.

D. H. Garrison, *Horace.* Epodes *and* Odes. *A New Annotated Latin Edition*. Norman, OK, 1991.

K. Quinn, *Horace. The* Odes. London, 1980.

OVID

C. A. Jestin and P. B. Katz, *Ovid.* Amores, Metamorphoses. *Selections*. Wauconda, 2000.

GENERAL

American Classical League, *Standards for Classical Language Learning*. Oxford, OH, 1997.

M. Balme and J. Morwood, *Oxford Latin Course. Part III*. Oxford, 1995.

R. Maltby, *Latin Love Elegy*. Wauconda, 1985.

C. A. Murphy, D. G. Thiem, and R. T. Moore, *Embers of the Ancient Flame. Latin Love Poetry. Selections from Catullus, Horace and Ovid*. Wauconda, 2001.

P. Rutherford, *Instructions for All Students*. Alexandria, VA, 1998.

GLOSSARY

PROPER NAMES

Amor, Amōris, *m.:* Cupid, Love

Antōnius, -a, -um: a Roman clan name; substantive: Antony, Marc Antony

Argīvus, -a, -um: pertaining to Argos, a city in the Peloponnese area of Greece; Argive, Greek

Atticus, -a, -um: Attic, Athenian; substantive: a man's name, Atticus

Caesar, -aris, *m.:* a common *cognomen* for several members of the *gēns Iūliāna,* the imperial family; Gaius Julius Caesar, politician, general, dictator

Calais, -is, *m.:* a name; the son of a man named Ornytus who lived in Thūriī, a town in southern Italy

Carthāgō, -inis, *f.:* name of a city in North Africa

Catullus, -ī, *m.:* a name; a poet from Verona, Gaius Valerius Catullus

Chloē, Chloes, *f.:* a (Greek) woman's name. The Greek word *chloē* means "green bud, twig, shoot."

Corinna, -ae, *f.:* a (Greek) woman's name

Cupīdō, -inis, *m.:* Cupid, Amor, the son of Venus

Cyprus, -ī, *f.:* an island in the Aegean Sea that was central to worship of Venus

Eurus, -ī, *m.:* the East Wind

Gaetūlus, -a, -um: Gaetulian. Gaetulia was an area in northwestern Africa renowned for its lions.

Germania, -ae, *f.:* Germany

Graecia, -ae, *f.:* Greece

Hadria, -ae, *m.:* the Adriatic Sea, located between Italy and Greece

Helvētius, -a, -um: Swiss, Helvetian

Herculēs, -is, *m.:* Hercules/Heracles, a demigod and hero of Greek myth

Īlia, -ae, *f.:* Ilia, also known as Rhea Silvia, the legendary mother of Romulus and Remus.

Ītalia, -ae, *f.:* Italy

Iuppiter, Iōvis, *m.:* Jupiter, king of the gods

Lais: the name of a Corinthian courtesan celebrated for her beauty

Latīnus, -a, -um: pertaining to Latium, an area in central Italy; Latin

Lȳdia, -ae, *f.* a woman's name mentioned in several of Horace's *Odes.* Since Lȳdia was also the name of a region along the western coast of Asia Minor, the name may reflect her origins. Cf. Adriana, Athena, Alexandra, Geneva or Paris as modern place-related names for women

Mars, Martis, *m.:* Mars, god of war

Memphis, -is, *f.:* a city in Egypt, site of temple to Venus and Pharaonic capital city

Pallas, -adis, *f.:* an epithet for Athena

Persa, -ae, *m.:* a Persian

Phoebus, -ī, *m.:* epithet for Apollo (as Sun god); sun

Publius, -ī, *m.:* a common Roman *praenomen*

Quintia, -ae, *f.:* a common Roman *praenomen*

Rhēsus, -ī, *m.:* a Thracian leader who brought his forces to fight on behalf of the Trojans against the Greeks

Rōmānus, -a, -um: Roman

Rōmulus, -ī, *m.:* co-founder and first king of Rome

Semīramis, -idis, *f.:* a name from the Near-East, especially associated with Assyria; a famous queen, builder of Babylon

Sīthonius, -a, -um: Sithonian. The Sīthoniī were a tribe in Thrace in northeastern Greece.

Thrēicius, -a,-um: Thracian, from Thrace in northeastern Greece

Thressus, -a, -um: Thracian, from Thrace in northeastern Greece

Venus, -eris, *f.:* Venus/Aphrodite, the goddess of Love and Beauty

LATIN-ENGLISH VOCABULARY

A

ā, ab: *prep. + abl:* agency: by; time: since, from, after; space: from, away from

abeō, abīre, abiī, abitum: *intr.* go away

accipiō, accipere, accēpī, acceptum: take to, receive, accept

accūsō, accūsāre, accūsāvī, accūsātum: blame; accuse, prosecute

ad: *prep. + acc.:* space: to, towards (motion); at, near (rest); time: toward, about, at, by; numbers: about, almost

adaperta: a variant of *aperta:* see *aperiō*

adeō, adīre, adiī, aditum: *intr.* go to, approach, visit

adpōnō: variant of *appōnō*

adulescēns, -centis, *m.:* young person, young man

adveniō, advenīre, advēnī, adventum: *intr.* come toward, arrive, approach.

adventus, -ūs, *m.:* an arrival, approach; a visit

adversus, -a, -um: opposing, obstructing, standing in the way; turned toward, facing, opposite

aegrē: *adv.:* with difficulty, barely

aēneus,-a, -um: bronze

aequus, -a, -um: even, level; fair, just, reasonable, equal; calm, flat, smooth

aestimō, aestimāre, aestimāvī, aestimātum: value, reckon

aestus, -ūs, *m.:* heat, sultriness

aetās, -tātis, *f.:* an age, lifetime; a period of life, a generation

afficiō, afficere, affēcī, affectum: treat, handle, manage; influence, move; attack; afflict

ager, agrī, *m.:* field, plot of ground; territory

agmen, -minis, *n.:* a marching column (of an army), army

agō, agere, ēgī, actum: do; drive, lead, conduct; discuss; spend (time); live (a life)

agricola, -ae, *m.:* a farmer

aliquis, aliquid: someone, something

alius, alia, aliud: other, another (of three or more)

alius . . . alius: one . . . another; aliī . . . aliī: some . . . others

alter, altera, alterum: the other (of two)

alter . . . alter: the one . . . the other

altus, -a, -um: high, tall; deep

amāns, amantis, *m.:* a loving one, a lover

ambō, ambae, ambō: both, the two

ambulō, ambulāre, ambulāvī, ambulātum: *intr.* walk, amble, march; traverse, travel

amīca, -ae, *f.:* a girlfriend; a mistress

amīcus, -ī, *m:* a friend; a boyfriend, a lover; a partisan, a supporter

āmittō, āmittere, āmīsī, āmissum: let go, release; let slip, miss; lose

amō, amāre, amāvī, amātum: love, like, be fond of, fall in love with

amor, amōris, *m.:* love, affection; fondness, attachment; strong desire, yearning

anima, -ae, *f.:* breath, spirit, life; darling

animus, -ī, *m.:* mind, soul, spirit; pl. may = morale, courage

ante: *adv.:* before, previously, in the past; in front of, forwards; *prep. + accus.:* before, in front of (space, time, preference)

antequam: *conj.:* before, sooner . . . than

antīquē: *adv.:* in former times

aperiō, aperīre, aperuī, apertum: open, spread apart

appōnō, appōnere, apposuī, appositum: put, lay, or set near, at, along side (+ dat)

aptus, -a, -um: fit, suitable, handy, ready, useful

aqua, -ae, *f.:* water

arbitror, arbitrārī, arbitrātus sum: think

arcus, -ūs, *m.:* bow

ardeō, ardēre, arsī, arsūrus: burn, be on fire (with passion)

arma, -ōrum, *n. pl.:* arms, weapons, armor

armō, armāre, armāvī, armātum: arm, rouse to arms

arrogāns (arrogantis): scornful, arrogant, proud, overbearing

artus, -ūs, *m.:* joint, limb

ās, assis, *m.:* an *as*, the smallest Roman coin

asper, -era, -erum: fierce, rough, wild, harsh, cruel

aspiciō, aspicere, aspexī, aspectum: look at, behold, lay eyes on

at: *conj.:* a emphatically adversative word, BUT

atque: *conj.:* and, and also, and even; than, as (in comparisons)

atquī: like *at*, a emphatically adversative word: AND YET, BUT

audeō, audēre, ausus sum: semideponent: dare (to)

audiō, audīre, audīvī, audītum: hear, listen to

aura, -ae, *f.:* breeze

auris, -is, *f.:* ear

aut: *conj.:* or

aut . . . aut: either . . . or

auxilium, -ī, *n.:* aid, help, relief, remedy

āvius, -a, -um: pathless, trackless, remote

B

barbitos, -ī, *m./f.:* Greek noun: a lyre, a lute

bāsiō, bāsiāre, bāsiāvī, bāsiātum: kiss

bāsium, -ī, *n:* kiss

beātus, -a, -um: blessed; happy; prosperous; fertile

bellum, -ī, *n.:* war

bellus, -a, -um: pretty, charming, handsome

bis: *adv.:* twice

bonus, -a, -um: good; cheerful (face); sound, valid (argument); pretty, shapely

bracchium, -ī, *n.:* arm, forearm (elbow to wrist)

brevis, -e: short (stature); short, brief, transient (time)

C

cadō, cadere, cecidī, casum: *intr.:* fall, sink, settle; die; happen, occur

caedō, caedere, cecīdī, caesum: cut, chop; strike, beat; kill, murder

caelestis, -e: heavenly, celestial; divine, supernatural

candidus, -a, -um: fair-skinned, white-complexioned

canō, canere, cecinī, cantum: sing; play (an instrument); prophesy

capiō, capere, cēpi, captum: seize, grasp; capture, take

careō, carēre, caruī, _____: lack, be without (+ abl.)

carrus, -ī, *m.:* cart, wagon; chariot, car

castīgātus, -a, -um: firm, disciplined, exercised, well-muscled

castra, -ōrum, *n. pl.:* a camp

caterva, -ae, *f.:* a squad, troop

causor, causārī, causātus sum: give or plead (the accus.) as an excuse or reason

centum: a hundred

certus, -a, -um: fixed, definite, sure; certain

cervix, cervīcis, *f.:* neck, nape of the neck

cēterus, -a, -um: other; the rest of, remaining

cibum, -ī, *n.:* food

cithara, -ae, *f.:* lyre

cīvis, -is, *m.:* citizen

clārus, -a, -um: clear, bright; famous, notorious

classis, -is, *f.:* fleet (of ships)

claudō, claudere, clausī, clausum: close, shut; conclude; lock up, imprison; limit, blockade

cōgō, cōgere, coēgī, coāctum: drive or gather together, collect; assemble; force, compel

collum, -ī, *n:* neck

coma, -ae, *f.:* hair

comparō, comparāre, comparāvī, comparātum: unite; match; compare

confiteor, confitērī, confessus sum: confess, admit, acknowledge; allow, grant

congerō, congerere, congessī, congestum: heap up, pile up

conor, conārī, conātus sum: try (to), attempt (to)

consilium, -ī, *n.:* plan, advice, counsel

constituō, constituere, constituī, constitūtum: decide (to), determine (to); settle, establish; set up, erect

consul, -sulis, *m.:* consul

conturbō, conturbāre, conturbāvī, conturbātum: thoroughly mix up, stir, confuse

conveniō, convenīre, convēnī, conventum: be suitable, fit, be appropriate, suit

cōpia, -ae, *f.:* supply, abundance; plenty, multitude; *pl.:* resources; troops

cor, cordis, *n.:* heart

cornū, -ūs, *n.:* horn, antler; wing (of an army)

corpus, -poris, *n.:* body, corpse

cortex, corticis, *m.:* a cork, piece of bark (or rind)

crās: *adv.:* tomorrow

crēdibilis, -e: credible, trustworthy, plausible, likely

crēdō, crēdere, crēdidī, crēditum: *tr.:* entrust (accus.) to (dat.); *intr.:* trust, believe in (+ dat.)

crepusculum, -ī, *n.:* twilight, dimness, obscurity; *pl.* may mean darkness

cum: *prep. + abl.:* with; *conj.:* when, since, although

cum prīmum: *conj.:* as soon as

cupīdō, cupīdinis, *f.:* desire, eagerness, greed; passion; lust

cupidus, -a,-um: desirous, eager

cupiō, cupere, cupīvī, cupītum: desire, want, wish for

cūr: *conj.:* why?

currō, currere, cucurrī, cursum: *intr.:* run

custōdiō, custōdīre, custōdīvī(or –iī), custōdītum: watch, guard, protect

custōs, -tōdis, *m.:* guard; watchman, sentinel

D

dēbeō, dēbēre, dēbuī, dēbitum: owe; ought (+ comple. infin.)

dēcipiō, dēcipere, dēcēpī, dēceptum: deceive, cheat; escape the notice of

dēfendō, dēfendere, dēfendī, dēfēnsum: defend, protect; guard; repel, avert, keep off

dēfungor, dēfungī, dēfunctus sum: *intr.:* be discharged, retired, done with, finished

deinde: *adv.:* then, next, afterwards

dēleō, dēlēre, dēlēvī, dēlētum: destroy

dēmānō, dēmānāre, dēmānāvī, _____: *intr.:* run/drip down, trickle, flow, spread

dēmonstrō, dēmonstrāre, dēmonstrāvī, dēmonstrātum: point out, show; demonstrate

densus, -a, -um: thick, heavy

dēpōnō, dēpōnere, dēposuī, dēpositum: put down, deposit; lay aside

deus, -ī, *m.:* god, deity

dēripiō, dēripere, dēripuī, dēreptum: snatch, tear, rip off or down

dēserō, dēserere, dēseruī, dēsertum: desert, abandon, forsake

dēsidia, -ae, *f.:* laziness, idleness, inactivity

dēsinō, dēsinere, dēsiī, dēsitum: stop, halt, cease (+ complementary infinitive)

destinātus, -a, -um: stubborn, fixed, determined, settled, having made up one's mind

dīcō, dīcere, dīxī, dictum: say; tell, relate; indicate, mention, specify

dīdūcō, dīdūcere, dīduxī, dīductum: separate, draw apart

diēs, diēī, *m.:* day

difficilis, -e: difficult, hard

digitus, -ī, *m.:* finger

dīligēns (dīligentis): careful, accurate; exacting, strict; industrious, diligent

dīmoveō, dīmovēre, dīmōvī, dīmōtum: move apart, separate; disperse; dismiss

discēdō, discēdere, discessī, discessum: *intr.:* go apart, go in different directions, depart, leave

discipulus, -ī, *m.:* student, pupil, learner, disciple

dīva, -ae, *f.:* goddess

dīves (dīvitis): rich, wealthy; as a substantive, a rich man

dīviduus, -a, -um: separated, divided

dīvus, -ī, *m.:* deity, god

dō, dare, dedī, datum: give, bestow

doceō, docēre, docuī, doctum: teach, instruct; tell, inform

doctus, -a, -um: learned, skilled, taught

doleō, dolēre, doluī, dolitum: *intr.:* suffer grief, pain or hurt

domesticus, -a, -um: of the house; domestic, household; familiar, private, personal

domina, -ae, *f.:* mistress, lady of the house, owner; sweetheart; wife

dominus, -ī, *m.:* master, lord, owner, proprietor; tyrant; commander; lover

domus, -ūs, *f.:* house, home

dōnec: *conj.:* so long as, while

dōnum, -ī, *n.:* gift, pesent; offering, sacrifice

dormiō, dormīre, dormīvī, dormītum: sleep

dubius, -a, -um: wavering, doubtful, uncertain

dūcō, dūcere, duxī, ductum: lead, guide

dulcis, -e: sweet; pleasant, delightful; dear, affectionate

dum: *conj.: w/indic.:* while, as long as; *w/subj.:* until; provided that, if only

duo, duae, duo: two

duplicō, duplicāre, duplicāvī, duplicātum: double

dūrō, dūrāre, dūrāvī, dūrātum: harden, solidify; inure, toughen

dūrus, -a, -um: hard, harsh, cruel

dux, ducis, *m.:* leader, guide; general, commander

E

ē, ex: *prep. + abl.:* out of, out from

ecce: *interj.:* Look! See! Lo! Lo and behold!

ego: *pers. pron.:* I

ēlectus, -a, -um: select, chosen, choice

ēlegans (ēlegantis): elegant; choosy, choice, fine, select

eō, īre, iī, itum: *intr.:* go

epistula, -ae, *f.:* letter, epistle

eques, equitis, *m.:* cavalryman, knight

equus, -ī, *m.:* horse, steed

ergō: *adv.:* therefore, consequently

ēripiō, ēripere, ēripuī, ēreptum: snatch out of, save, rescue; pull out, tear out

errō, errāre, errāvī, errātum: wander, stray, roam; miss the mark, err

et: *conj.:* and

et . . . et: both . . . and

etiam: *adv.:* even; also

excēdō, excēdere, excessī, excessum: *intr.:* go out, depart, leave

excutiō, excutere, excussī, excussum: shake out, extinguish, cast out, jilt

exercitus, -ūs, *m.:* army, trained band

exigō, exigere, exēgī, exactum: drive out

eximō, eximere, exēmī, exemptum: take away, remove

experiēns (experientis): active, enterprising

exterō, exterere, extrīvī, extrītum: rub out, wear away, trample

exūrō, exūrere, exussī, exustum: burn; dry up; consume, destroy; purge; inflame

F

facilis, -e: doable, easy

faciō, facere, fēcī, factum: do, make

fāmōsus, -a, -um: much talked of, famous, renowned; infamous; slanderous, libelous

fās: *indecl.: n.:* divine law, sacred duty; divine will, fate; right, natural law

fātum, -ī, *n.:* fate, destiny

fax, facis, *f.:* torch, fire-brand, taper

fēmina, -ae, *f.:* woman, female

femur, femoris, *n.:* thigh

fenestra, -ae, *f.:* window

ferē: *adv.:* generally, usually, as a rule

ferō, ferre, tulī, lātum: bear, endure; carry

ferus, -a, -um: fierce, savage; wild, untamed

fīdēs, fideī, *f.:* faith, trust, loyalty

fīdūcia, -ae, *f.:* trust, confidence; reliability, trustworthiness; self-confidence

fīlia, -ae, *f.:* daughter

fīlius, -ī, *m.:* son

fīnis, -is, *m.:* end, limit, boundary, border; *pl:* territory

fiō, fierī, (factus sum): be made, be done, happen

flagellum, -ī, *n.:* lash, whip

flamma, -ae, *f.:* flame

flāvus, -a, -um: reddish-blonde, flame-colored, fiery

flūmen, -minis, *n.:* river, stream

folium, -ī, *n.:* leaf, foliage

fore: a variant of futūrus, -a, -um esse

foris, -is, *m.:* a door, gate, entrance; *pl.:* a set of double-doors, i.e. two side-by-side panels which made up the *ianua*

forma, -ae, *f.:* form, shape, figure; beauty, good looks

formōsus, -a, -um: shapely, physically attractive/beautiful

fortis, -e: brave, strong

forum, -ī, *n.:* marketplace, forum

frangō, frangere, frēgī, fractum: break, crush, maul

frāter, -tris, *m.:* brother

fretum, -ī, *n.:* strait, sea

frīgus, -goris, *n.:* cold, chill, frost

frūmentum, -ī, *n.:* grain

fruor, fruī, fructus sum: *intr.:* enjoy, delight in (+ abl.)

fugiō, fugere, fūgī, fugitum: *intr.:* flee

fugitīvus, -ī, *m.:* fugitive, runaway, escapee

funāle, -is, *n.:* torch

fungor, fungī, functus sum: *intr.:* perform; busy oneself with; finish; complete (+ abl.)

G

geminus, -a, -um: twin

gēns, gentis, *f.:* family, clan, nation

genū, -ūs, *n.:* knee

genus, generis, *n.:* type, class, sort, kind

gerō, gerere, gessī, gestum: carry on; wear; wage

glōria, -ae, *f.:* glory, fame, renown

gradior, gradī, gressus sum: move, go

grātia, -ae, *f.:* grace, charm, loveliness; favor, kindness; thanks, gratitude

grātus, -a, -um: pleasing, welcome; grateful (+ dat.)

gravis, -e: heavy, weighty; stern, severe

H

habeō, habēre, habuī, habitum: have, hold; consider, deem

habilis, -e: handy, suitable, fit

herī: *adv.:* yesterday, in the past

hic, haec, hoc: *demon. adj.:* this

hīc: *adv.:* here, in this place; at this point

hodiē: *adv.:* today

homō, hominis, *m.:* human, human being, man

hōra, -ae, *f.:* hour

hostis, -is, *m.:* foe, an enemy; *pl.:* the enemy

humānus, -a, -um: human

I

iaceō, iacēre, iacuī, _____: lie open, be flat

iaciō, iacere, iēcī, iactum: throw, cast, hurl

iam: *adv.:* now, already, soon

iānua, -ae, *f.:* door, entrance

identidem: *adv.:* repeatedly, again and again

idōneus, -a, -um: fit, suitable, able-bodied, appropriate (+ dative)

ignis, -is, *f.:* fire

ille, illa, illud: *demon. adj.:* that (over there), that (of him, her, it, them)

ille . . . hic: the former . . . the latter

imber, imbris, *m.:* rainstorm, rain; sometimes hail, snow

imperātor, -tōris, *m.:* commander, general

imperium, -ī, *n.:* authority, power to command; dominion, sway; empire; command, order

impetus, -ūs, *m.:* force, attack, onslaught

improbus, -a, -um: uneven, rough, stormy, troublesome

in: *prep. + acc.:* into, onto, against; + *abl.:* in, on

inaequus, -a, -um: uneven, unlevel, unfair; unjust, unreasonable, unequal; uncalm, unsmooth

incohō, -āre, -āvī, -ātum: begin

ineō, inīre, iniī, initum: go in, enter

ineptiō, ineptīre, _____, _____: *intr.:* be absurd, make a fool of oneself

inermis, -e: unarmed, defenseless

infacētus, -a, um: dull, crude, lacking wit/humor; witless, clueless

infestus, -a, -um: hostile, deadly

ingenium, -ī, *n.:* intellect, character, spirit, nature

inhorrescō, inhorrescere, inhorruī, _____: begin to tremble, quiver, shake; i.e. rustle, make a rustling sound; begin to bristle

insapiēns (insapientis): unwise, tasteless

insidiae, -ārum, *f. pl.:* plot, ambush

instruō, instruere, instruxī, instructum: build up, construct; furnish, provide; instruct; deploy (mil. usage)

intellegō, intellegere, intellexī, intellectum: understand, perceive, comprehend; realize, recognize

inuleus, -ī, *m.:* a fawn, young deer

invādō, invādere, invāsī, invāsum: go into, enter; undertake, attempt; invade, rush upon; seize, take possession of

inveniō, invenīre, invēnī, inventum: come upon, find, discover

invideō, invidēre, invīdī, invīsum: be jealous of, envy; put the evil eye on, bewitch

invītus, -a, -um: unwilling, against one's will

ipse, ipsa, ipsum: *intensive adj.:* _____self, very

īra, -ae, *f.:* anger, wrath

īrācundus, -a, -um: easily upset, irascible, prone to anger, hot-tempered, passionate

is, ea, id: *unemphatic demon.:* this, that (the one just mentioned or about to be mentioned); as a substantive: he, she, it.

iste, ista, istud: that (near you, of yours)

ita: *adv.:* so, thus, in such a way

iubeō, iubēre, iussi, iussum: order, bid

iūcundus, -a, -um: pleasant, delightful, agreeable

iūdicō, iūdicāre, iūdicāvī, iūdicātum:

iugum, -ī, *n.:* yoke, bond

iuvenālis, -e: youthful, juvenile

iuvenis, -is, *m.:* young man, youth

L

labellum, -ī, *n:* the diminuitive of *labrum:* little lip

labor, labōris, *m.:* effort; work, labor; trouble, distress, suffering

labōrō, labōrāre, labōrāvī, labōrātum: *tr.:* work at, produce; *intr.:* work; struggle, suffer, be hard pressed, be troubled

lacerta, -ae, *f.:* a lizard

lacertus, -ī, *m.:* (upper) arm, i.e. elbow to shoulder

laevus, -a, -um: left

lassus, -a, -um: weary, tired, worn-out, spent

latebrae, -ārum, *f.:* hiding places

lātus, -a, -um: wide, broad

latus, lateris, *n.:* side, flank

laudābilis, -e: praiseworthy, laudable

laudō, laudāre, laudāvī, laudātum: praise, laud

lēgātus, -ī, *m.* deputy; ambassador, envoy; lieutenant

legō, legere, lēgī, lēctum: gather; choose, pick; read

leō, leōnis, *m/f.:* lion

levis,-e: light, slight, quick (to change)

levō, levāre, levāvī, levātum: lift, raise, lighten, relieve, ease

lēx, lēgis, *f.:* law

libēns (libentis): willing, ready, glad

liber, -bri, *m.:* book

līberō, līberāre, līberāvī, līberātum: free, set free

līmen, -minis, *n.:* threshold, doorway, entrance; onset, beginning

lingua, -ae, *f.:* tongue, language

locus, -ī, *m.:* place, site

longus, -a, -um: long

loquor, loquī, locūtus sum: say, speak

lūcidus, -a, um: bright, full of light, glowing, burning

lūdō, lūdere, lūsī, lūsum: play, sport; mock, deride

lūmen, -minis, *n.:* light

lux, lūcis, *f.:* light

M

magis: *adv.:* more

magister, -trī, *m.:* master, teacher

magnus, -a, -um: large, great

maior, maius: comparative of *magnus, -a, -um:* larger, greater

mālō, malle, māluī, _____: wish more, prefer (+ complementary infinitive)

malus, -a, -um: bad, evil

maneō, manēre, mansī, mansum: *intr.:* remain, stay

manus, -ūs, *f.:* hand; handful, band (of soldiers)

mare, -is, *n.:* sea, ocean

marīnus, -a, -um: pertaining to the sea, marine

marītus, -ī, *m.:* husband, spouse

māter, mātris, *f.:* mother

medius, -a, -um: middle (of), midst (of)

membrum, -brī, *n.:* limb, member

menda, -ae, *f.:* flaw, blemish, fault

meridiēs, -diēī, *m.:* noon

-met: *intensive suffix:* -self, very

metuō, metuere, metuī, metūtum: fear, be afraid of, dread

metus, -ūs, *m.:* fear, dread

meus, -a, -um: my, mine

mīca, -ae, *f.:* crumb, morsel; grain (of sand)

mīles, mīlitis, *m.:* soldier

mīlia, -ium, *n. pl.:* thousands

mīlitō, mīlitāre, mīlitāvī, mīlitātum: to be a soldier

mille: *indeclinable adj.:* thousand

minax (minācis): threatening, menacing (+ dative)

minimus, -a, -um: superl. of *parvus;* smallest, least

misceō, miscēre, miscuī, mixtum: mix, mingle

miser, -era, -erum: wretched, unhappy, sad, miserable, poor

mittō, mittere, mīsī, missum: send; let go of; free, release

mōbilis, -e: mobile; movable, portable; nimble, active

modus, -ī, *m.:* (musical) measure, rhythm; the *pl.* can mean "poetry."

molestus, -a, -um: annoying, troublesome, distressing

moneō, monēre, monuī, monitum: remind, warn, counsel

mons, montis, *m.:* mountain

mordeō, mordēre, momordī, morsum: bite, nip, nibble on

morior, morī, mortuus sum: die, perish

mōs, mōris, *m.:* custom, habit; *pl.:* character

moveō, movēre, mōvī, mōtum: move

mox: *adv.:* soon

mulier, mulieris, *f.:* woman

multus, -a, -um: much, many a; *pl.:* many

mūtuus, -a, -um: shared, mutual, reciprocal

N

nam: *conj.:* for

narrō, narrāre, narrāvī, narrātum: *trans.:* relate, tell, narrate, recount; *intr.:* speak, tell

nāsus, -ī, *m.:* nose

navigō, navigāre, navigāvī, navigātum: *intr.:* sail

-ne: enclitic indicating a neutral question, i.e. one to which the answer may be "yes" or "no"

nē: *conj.:* so that . . . not, lest

negō, negāre, negāvī, negātum: deny, say . . . no

nēmō, nēminis, *m.:* no one, nobody

nempe: *adv.:* to be sure, certainly, surely, without any doubt

neque (nec): and . . . not, nor

neque (nec) . . . neque (nec): neither . . . nor

nesciō, nescīre, nescīvī, nescītum: not to know

niger, -gra, -grum: dark, swarthy, black

nihil (nil): *indecl.:* *n.:* nothing

nimbus, -ī, *m.:* cloudburst, rainstorm

nimis: *adv.:* too, excessively

nisi: *conj.:* if . . . not, unless

nix, nivis, *f.:* snow

noceō, nocēre, nocuī, nocitum: harm, injure (+ dative).

nōlō, nolle, nōluī, _____: be unwilling, not want (+ comple. inf.)

nōmen, -minis, *n.:* name,

nōn: *adv.:* not

nōn iam: *adv.:* no longer

nōn sōlum (modo) . . . sed etiam: not only . . . but also

nōs: *pers. pron.:* we

noster, tra, -trum: our

nox, noctis, *f.:* night

nūbō, nūbere, nupsī, nuptum: wed, marry (+ dat.)

nūdus, -a, -um: bare, nude, undressed

nūga, -ae, *f.:* a trifling, a scrap; a scribbling

nullus, -a, -um: not any, no, none

numerus, -ī, *m.:* number, numeral

nunc: *adv.:* now

nuntius, -ī, *m.:* announcer, messenger; announcement, message

nūper: *adv.:* recently, lately, not long ago

nusquam: *adv.:* nowhere, on no occasion

O

obdūrō, obdūrāre, obdūrāvī, obdūrātum: be hard against, stand out, persist, be firm, be tough

obeō, obīre, obiī, obitum: die; *mortem obīre:* go to (meet) death, die

obsideō, obsidēre, obsēdī, obsessum: lay siege to, besiege

occidō, occidere, occidī, occāsum: set, sink, fall

occīdō, occīdere, occīsī, occīsum: cut, cut down, strike, slay

ocellus, -ī, *m.:* a diminuitive form of *oculus, -ī, m.:* little eye

officium, -ī, *n.:* duty, task, office

omnis, -e: each, every; *pl.:* all

oportet, oportēre, oportuit: it is proper, it is right, it is necessary; one should

oppidum, -ī, *n.:* town

oppōnō, oppōnere, opposuī, oppositum: hinder, oppose, block

ops, opis, *f.:* power, might; help, aid; *pl.:* wealth, resources

opus, operis, *n.:* product of work, work; deed, task; work of art

ōrātor, -tōris, *m.:* speaker, orator

orior, orīrī, ortus sum: arise, rise

ōs, ōris, *n.:* mouth; *pl.* face, countenance

ōtium, -ī, *n.:* leisure

P

papilla, -ae, *f.:* breast

pār (pāris) (+ dative): equal, like

parcō, parcere, pepercī, parsūrus: *intr.:* spare, forebear, refrain from injuring (+ dative)

pariēs, parietis, *m.:* a (house) wall

parō, parāre, parāvī, parātum: get, get ready, prepare

pars, partis, *f.:* part; faction; direction (part of the compass)

parvus, a-, -um: small, little

pateō, patēre, patuī, _____: lie flat, lie low; extend

pater, patris, *m.:* father

patior, patī, passus sum: suffer, permit, allow; endure, bear

patria, -ae, *f.:* homeland, fatherland, country

paucī, -ae, -a: few

pavidus, -a, -um: quaking, trembling (with fear)

pax, pācis, *f.:* peace; peace treaty; compact, treaty; pardon (from the gods)

pectus, -toris, *n.:* chest, breast, heart

pecūnia, -ae, *f.:* money, sum of money

perferō, perferre, pertulī, perlātum: bear through, suffer, undergo, endure

perīculum, -ī, *n.:* danger, peril, risk

perpetuus, -a, -um: eternal, perpetual, everlasting

persequor, persequī, persecūtus sum: hunt, pursue, track, punish, avenge

perveniō, pervenīre, pervēnī, perventum: *intr.:* come through to, arrive at, reach

pervigilō, pervigilāre, pervigilāvī, pervigilātum: keep watch, be on guard all night

pēs, pedis, *m.:* foot, paw

pessimus, -a, -um: superl. of *malus:* worst, most evil

petō, petere, petīvī, petītum: seek, aim at; attack (a person)

pius, -a, -um: dutiful, loyal, true

plānus, -a, -um: flat, level, even

poēma, poēmatis, *n.:* poem; poetry

poena, -ae, *f.:* penalty, punishment

polliceor, pollicērī, pollicitus sum: promise

pōnō, pōnere, posuī, positum: put, place

populus, -ī, *m.:* population, populace; a people

porta, -ae, *f.:* gate, entrance; outlet

portō, portāre, portāvī, portātum: carry

possum, posse, potuī, _____: be able (to), can (+ compl. infin.)

post: *prep. + accus.:* after, behind

postquam: *conj.:* after

potior, potīrī, potītus sum: gain possession of, possess (+ abl. or sometimes gen.)

potior, -ius: more able, more powerful, preferable, better

praebeō, praebēre, praebuī, praebitum: offer, provide, supply, present

premō, premere, pressī, pressum: press, squeeeze

priscus, -a, -um: old, former, ancient

priusquam: *conj.:* before; until

prō: *prep. + abl.:* before, in front of; for, on behalf of; for, instead of

prōditiō, -iōnis, *f.:* betrayal, treason

proelium, -ī, *n.:* battle, fight, combat

prōpōnō, -ere, prōposuī, prōpositum: put forward, propose, suggest, offer

prōsum, prōdesse, prōfuī, prōfutūrus: be advantageous, helpful, useful to (+ dat.)

prōveniō, prōvenīre, prōvenī, prōventum: *intr.:* come forth, proceed; come out, appear; come about, happen

prōvincia, -ae, *f.:* province, sphere of action or office

pūblicus, -a, -um: public, pertaining to the people or state

pudor, pudōris, *m.:* (sexual) shame, modesty, decency, propriety

puella, -ae, *f.:* girl, girlfriend, sweetheart

puer, -ī, *m.:* boy, lad; servant, slave; bachelor

pugnō, pugnāre, pugnāvī, pugnātum: *intr.:* fight; contend, dispute; *tr.:* struggle with, oppose, fight against

pulcher, -chra, -chrum: beautiful, fair, handsome

putō, putāre, putāvī, putātum: think, ponder, consider, judge; suppose, imagine; reckon, estimate, value

Q

quaerō, quaerere, quaesīvī, quaesītum: ask, inquire; seek, search for; try to gain, earn, acquire

quālis, -e: of what sort or kind?

quāliter: *adv.:* as, just as; in like fashion, just like

quam: *adv.:* how, than, as

quamquam: *conj.:* although

quantus, -a, -um: how great, how much, of what size, of what importance, of what worth?

-que: *enclitic:* and

-que . . . -que: both . . . and

quīcumque, quaecumque, quodcumque: *rel and indef. pron. and adj.:* whoever, whatever

quis, quid: *inter. pron.:* who, what?; *indef. pron.* (with *sī, nisi, nē, num*): anyone, anything

quisquam, quidquam: *indef. adj.:* any, some

quoad: *adv.:* to what extent, how far? by what time, how soon? how long?; *conj.:* while, as long as

quondam: *adv.:* formerly, at one time, once; someday, one day

quoque: *adv.:* (follows word it emphasizes): too, also

R

rapidus, -a, -um: tearing away, seizing; fierce, consuming; rapid, swift, rushing, impetuous

rārus, -a, -um: thin, scanty i.e. filmy, gauzy

recingō, recingere, recinxī, recinctum: unfasten, untie, undo, loosen, take off

rectus, -a, -um: straight-backed, having a good posture/carriage

redeō, redīre, rediī, reditum: *intr.:* go back, return, revert to

referō, referre, rettulī, relātum: bring back, renew, repeat; announce, report, relate, tell

rēgīna, -ae, *f.:* queen

regō, regere, rexī, rectum: rule, govern; guide, conduct; manage, direct

reiciō, reicere, reiēcī, reiectum: throw back, drive back, reject

remittō, remittere, remīsī, remissum: send back, return, restore

requiescō, requiescere, requiēvī, requiētum: *trans.:* begin to put to rest; *intrans.:* begin to rest or quiet down; relax, find peace

requīrō, requīrere, requīsīvī, requīsītum: ask back, seek again

rēs, reī, *f.:* thing, matter, affair, situation

resurgō, resurgere, resurrexī, resurrectum: *intr.:* rise or appear again

reveniō, revenīre, revēnī, reventum: *intr.:* come again or back, return

rex, rēgis, *m.:* king, ruler; patron

rīdeō, rīdēre, rīsī, rīsum: laugh, smile

rīvālis, -is, *m.:* one who uses the same stream, a neighbor; one who "uses" the same mistress, a rival

rogō, rogāre, rogāvī, rogātum: ask, inquire, request

rubus, -ī, *m.:* a bramble-bush, blackberry

rūmor, -mōris, *m.:* gossip, rumor; fame, notoriety

S

saeculum, -ī, *n.:* age, generation

saepe: *adv.:* often

sāl, salis, *m.:* salt, seasoning, flavor; good taste, elegance; wit, humor, sarcasm

salveō, salvēre, ____, ____: be well, be in good health

sanctus, -a, -um: consecrated, sacred, holy

sanē: *adv.:* really, indeed, to be sure

sānus, -a, -um: sound, hale, healthy; sane, rational, sensible; sober

sapiēns (sapientis): wise, sensible, judicious, discreet; as a substantive: a philospher, a sage

sapientia, -ae, *f.:* wisdom; common sense; knowledge

scelestus, -a, -um: wicked, evil, accursed, infamous

sciō, scīre, scīvī, scītum: know; realize, understand

scrībō, scrībere, scrīpsī, scrīptum: write, compose, draft

scrīptum, -ī, *n.:* writing, composition, treatise, book

secundus, -a, -um: second, following; favorable, supporting

sed: *conj.:* but; but also

sedeō, sedēre, sēdī, sessum: *intr.:* sit, be seated; be idle, be inactive

semel: *adv.:* once, once and for all

semper: *adv.:* always, ever

senātus, -ūs, *m.:* senate

senex, (senis): old, elderly; as a substantive, old man, codger

senīlis, -e: of an old man, aged, senile

sensus, -ūs, *m.:* sensation, sense; consciousness; awareness

sequor, sequī, secūtus sum: follow, ensue; escort, go with; chase

servitūs, -tūtis, *f.:* slavery, servitude

servō, servāre, servāvī, servātum: save, guard, preserve, keep

servus, -ī, *m.:* servant, slave

seu: *conj.:* or if, or

seu . . . seu: whether . . . or, if . . . or if

sevērus, -a, -um: stern, strict, austere

sī: *conj.:* if

sīc: *adv.:* thus, so, in this way; thus, in such a way

siccus -a, -um: dry, arid, parched

sīdus, sīderis, *n.:* a star, constellation

signum, -ī, *n.:* sign, signal; military standard, banner

silva, -ae, *f.:* forest, wood

similis, -e: like, similar

simul: *adv.:* at the same time

simul atque (ac): *conj.:* as soon as

sine: *prep. w/ abl.:* without

singulī, -ae, -a: one-by-one, individual; single, one at a time

sinister, -tra, -trum: left, on the left; unfavorable, unlucky

sīve (seu) . . . sīve (seu): if . . . or if, whether . . . or

socius, -ī, *m.:* partner, companion, ally

sōl, sōlis, *m.:* sun, sunlight, sunshine; day

soleō, solēre, solitus sum: be accustomed (to)

sōlus, -a, -um: alone, only, single

somnus, -ī, *m.:* sleep; night; sleep of death

sonitus, -ūs, *m.:* sound, noise

sopiō, sopīre, sopīvī, sopītum: put to sleep, stun, knock unconscious

sopōrātus, -a, -um: sound asleep, buried in sleep, unconscious

spectō, spectāre, spectāvī, spectātum: look at, watch, observe

speculātor, -tōris, *m.:* spy, scout

spērō, spērāre, spērāvī, spērātum: hope, hope for, expect, look forward to, await

stō, stāre, stetī, statum: *intr.:* stand (still); stand firm, last, endure

strenuus, -a, -um: restless, keen, vigorous

studeō, studēre, studuī, _____: desire, be eager for (+ dat.); study

studium, ī, *n.:* eagerness, enthusiasm; study

stultus, -a, -um: foolish, stupid, silly

sub: *prep. w/abl.:* under, beneath, at the foot of; *w/acc.:* up to the foot of, up to

subitō: *adv.:* suddenly

sublīmis, -e: raised, uplifted

sublūceō, sublūcēre, _____, _____: *intr.:* shine faintly, shimmer, glimmer

suī: *3rd pers. reflexive pron.:* himself, herself, itself, themselves

sum, esse, fuī, futūrus: be

superō, superāre, superāvī, superātum: be above, surpass

superstes (superstitis): standing over, surviving, outliving

supersum, superesse, superfuī, superfutūrus: be left over, to survive

surripiō, surripere, surripuī, surreptum: steal, take away, filch

suus, -a, -um: *reflex. possessive adj.:* the 3rd person subject's own: his own, her own, its own, their own

T

tam: *adv.:* to such an extent/degree, so, so much

tamen: *adv.:* nevertheless, yet, still

tamquam: *conj.:* just as; just as if

tandem: *adv.:* expressing considerable impatience: finally, once and for all

tangō, tangere, tetigī, tactum: touch

tantum . . . quantum: as much . . . as, as large (great) . . . as

tantus, -a, -um: so large, so great

tardipēs (tardipedis): limping, lame, slowfooted

tegō, tegere, texī, tectum: cover, protect, shelter, hide

tēlum, -ī, *n.:* weapon, spear, javelin, dart

tempestīvus, -a, um: seasonable, fit, ripe, timely, mature (+ dative)

templum, -ī, *n.:* temple, shrine, sanctuary

temptō, temptāre, temptāvī, temptātum: test, try, attempt

tempus, temporis, *n.:* time, period, season; opportunity, occasion

teneō, tenēre, tenuī, tentum: hold, seize, grasp

tenuis, -e: thin, slender

terra, -ae, *f.:* earth, land, soil

terreō, terrēre, terruī, territum: scare, frighten, terrify

thalamus, -ī, *m.:* bedroom

tigris, -is, *m/f.:* tiger/tigress

timeō, timēre, timuī, _____: fear, be afraid

timidus, -a, um: timid, fearful, cowardly; afraid of (+ gen.)

tintinnō, tintinnāre, _____, _____: *intr.:* make a ringing sound, to ring

torpeō, torpēre, torpuī, _____: *intr.:* be paralyzed or numb

torreō, torrēre, torruī, tostum: burn, parch (with heat)

torus, -ī, *m.:* couch, bed

tōtus, -a, -um: whole, entire

trans: *prep. + accus.:* across

transeō, transīre, transiī, transitum: go across, cross over, go over

tremō, tremere, tremuī, _____: tremble, shiver, quake

trēs, tria: three

tū: *pers. pron.:* you (sg.)

tum . . . tum: not only . . . but also

tumidus, -a, -um: swollen, swelling, causing swells (waves)

tunica, -ae, *f.:* tunic

turpis, -e: ugly, loathsome, repulsive, shameful, disgusting

tyrannus, -ī, *m.:* absolute ruler, tyrant

U

ubi/ubī: *rel. and interog. adv.:* where

umerus, -ī, *m.:* shoulder

umquam: *adv.:* ever, at any time

ūnus, -a, -um: one

urbs, urbis, *f.:* city

usque: *adv.:* all the way

ut: *conj.: w/ indic.:* as, when, since; *w/subj.:* that, so that; how

uterque, utraque, utrumque: each (of two)

ūtor, ūtī, ūsus sum: *intr.:* use, employ (+ ablative)

V

vae: *interjection:* woe! damn!

valeō, valēre, valuī, valitūrus: *intr.:* be well, be strong, fare well; be powerful, be capable

vānus, -a, -um: empty, vacant; groundless, pointless; unreal, false; boastful, vain

-ve: *an enclitic:* or

-ve . . . -ve: either . . . or

vectis, -is, *m.:* a lever, crowbar, pry-bar

vel: *adv.:* even, actually; perhaps; or

vel . . . vel: either . . . or

vēlāmen, -minis, *n.:* clothing, garment, veil

vēlō, vēlāre, vēlāvī, vēlātum: veil, cover, dress, clothe

veniō, venīre, vēnī, ventum: *intr.:* come

venter, ventris, *m.:* belly, tummy, stomach

ventus, -ī, *m.:* wind

venus, veneris, *f.:* beauty, charm; intercourse, sex; love

venustās, -tātis, *f.:* charm, grace, beauty, loveliness, Venus-like quality

venustus, -a, -um: charming, graceful, lovely, beautiful

vēr, vēris, *n.:* spring (season)

verbum,-ī, *n.:* word

verēcundus, -a, -um: shy, bashful, modest, reserved

vēritās, -tātis, *f.:* truth; honesty, integrity

verrō, verrere, verrī, versum: pass over, skim, sweep, scour, row (over the waters)

versus, -ūs, *m.:* a verse, a line (of verse)

vescor, vescī, _____: *intr.:* feed on, eat, feast on; enjoy (+ abl.)

vester, -tra, -trum: your

via, -ae, *f.:* way, road, street

videō, vidēre, vīdī, vīsum: see, look at; understand, realize

videor, vidērī, vīsus sum: seem (to), seem best (to)

vigeō, vigēre, viguī, _____: flourish, thrive, be vigorous

vigil, vigilis, *m.:* a watchman, sentinel, guard

vincō, vincere, vīcī, victum: overcome, defeat, conquer

violō, -āre, -āvī, ātum: violate; harm by violence, outrage

vir, -ī, *m.:* man; hero; husband

viridis, -e: green, fresh, young, lively, vigorous

vīta, -ae, *f.:* life

vītō, vītāre, vītāvī, vītātum: avoid, shun

vīvō, vīvere, vīxī, vīctum: *intr.:* live, be alive

vocō, vocāre, vocāvī, vocātum: call, shout

volō, velle, voluī, _____: wish; intr: be willing (+ compl. inf.)

volō, volāre, volāvī, volātum: fly

vōs: *pers. pron.:* you (pl.)

voveō, vovēre, vōvī, vōtum: vow, promise

vox, vōcis, *f.:* voice

vulgus, vulgī, *n.:* common people; herd, flock; rabble, populace

vulnerō, vulnerāre, vulnerāvī, vulnerātum: wound

FOR INTERNATIONAL BACCALAUREATE AND COLLEGE

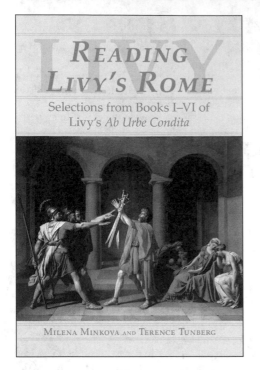

READING LIVY'S ROME
Selections from Books I–VI of Livy's *Ab Urbe Condita*

Milena Minkova and Terence Tunberg

Student Text: xii + 276 pp., 6 b&w illus. (2005)
6" x 9" Paperback,
ISBN 978-0-86516-550-2

Teacher's Guide: vi + 114 pp. (2005)
6" x 9" Paperback,
ISBN 978-0-86516-600-4

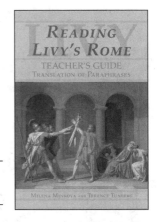

EASE STUDENTS INTO READING LIVY'S HISTORY

High-interest graded readings from Books I–VI of Livy's *Ab Urbe Condita*: Romulus and Remus, Cincinnatus, and more. Paraphrases with vocabulary stand opposite simplified and annotated Livian passages. Readings progress to authentic Livian passages, annotated but with fewer vocabulary aids. Appendix of authentic Livian passages for all simplified selections.

Features: • Simple Latin paraphrases for pre-reading • Extensive same-page glossaries • Inserts on features of Livy's language • English section titles for easy context • Graduated Livian Latin passages • Graduated notes on syntax and grammar • Full vocabulary

Teacher's Guide Features: literal translation of the paraphrases

I was expecting a text with which to transport intermediate Latin students beyond grammar drills into the place where practice begins to pay off the reading of a "real" author. I hoped for a work which would honor the intelligent student's thirst for a literary experience while still providing some lexical and syntactical assistance. In *Reading Livy's Rome* I have not been disappointed.

You will find all the old favorites here: Romulus and Remus, Coriolanus, Lucretia and Camillus. I was a little disappointed at the absence of Virginia (although Minkova and Tunberg have included the Twelve Tables), and the heroic cackling of Juno's geese is left out of the Gaulish Sack. Were I making the selections, I think I would have omitted the Licinio-Sextian Rogations, considering the amount of sociological background with which students will have to be provided to put them in an historical context. Such prejudices aside, however, let me say that I am delighted with the book's format, and I am convinced that my second-year students are fortunate in being able to begin their study of Latin literature with this text.

–Diane Johnson
Western Washington University

BOLCHAZY-CARDUCCI PUBLISHERS, INC.
WWW.BOLCHAZY.COM